D0287515

"King of the Wildcatters"

NUMBER NINE:
*Kenneth E. Montague Series
in Oil and Business History*
Joseph A. Pratt
General Editor

Thomas B. Slick, 1925. Courtesy Western History Collections, University of Oklahoma Library

"King of the Wildcatters"

of the

THE LIFE AND TIMES OF TOM SLICK, 1883–1930

Ray Miles

Texas A&M University Press
College Station

Copyright © 1996 by Ray Miles
Manufactured in the United States of America
All rights reserved
Second printing, 2004

The paper used in this book meets the minimum requirements
of the American National Standard for Permanence
of Paper for Printed Library Materials, Z39.48-1984.
Binding materials have been chosen for durability.
♾

Library of Congress Cataloging-in-Publication Data

Miles, Ray.
    "King of the wildcatters" : the life and times of Tom Slick, 1883–1930 /
Ray Miles.
       p.   cm.—(Kenneth E. Montague series in oil and business history ; 9)
    ISBN 0-89096-715-6 (alk. paper); ISBN 1-58544-399-9 (pbk.)
    1. Slick, Tom, 1883–1930. 2. Petroleum industry and trade—United
States—History. 3. Petroleum engineers—United States—Biography.
4. Petroleum conservation—United States—History.   I. Title.
II. Series: Kenneth E. Montague series in oil and business history ; no. 9.
HD9570.S55M55   1996
622'.3382'092—dc20
[B]   96-20128
                                          CIP

*This book is dedicated to
my mentor and friend,
ARRELL MORGAN GIBSON,
who deepened my respect for
writers and the love of books,
and to my grandmother
MARY MILES,
who taught me through her
example that most of the truly
important things in life
are not learned in books.*

Contents

Illustrations

Preface

Tom Slick was indeed an enigma. After he discovered oil at Cushing, Oklahoma, in 1912, the newspapers and oil trade journals of the day constantly followed his business endeavors, but he strenuously resisted all efforts by the public to learn more of his personal life. As he bluntly put it, "I'm not going to tell you anything about him." Writing a biography of someone who did not want anyone to know anything about him has presented problems.

The primary difficulty was getting a feel for his personality. Since he left extraordinarily few personal papers I have had to rely on other sources. Betty Slick Moorman, his daughter; Clifford L. Frates, his brother-in-law; and Ramona Frates Seeligson, his sister-in-law, have given me much insight into his character. Several newspaper articles, plus an interview that Slick had with a reporter from the *Kansas City Star,* provided a great deal of valuable information. (I would like to thank Loren Coleman for bringing that interview, by reporter A. B. MacDonald, to my attention.)

Following Slick's business trail presented special challenges as well. He left few business records. Accounts of his business methods and manners have been gleaned from numerous newspaper articles and from personal interviews with relatives, business associates, and former employees. Most of Slick's activities, however, have been pieced together from drilling reports found in the *Oil and Gas Journal.* Reading the reports from 1910 to 1930, I located all of

Slick's wells. From this information I constructed a chronology, using newspaper files to get a fuller accounting of his activities. All the small-town newspapers easily recognized the economic impact of an oil boom and were eager to report on the progress of wells. Literally hundreds of articles reported in minute detail Tom Slick's business trail throughout the Mid-Continent oil field. Slick's "paper trail" also led through courthouses where lease records and lawsuits were filed.

A biography of Tom Slick reveals much about the operation of independent oilmen from 1910 to 1930. This was a time of phenomenal change as explorers tried to locate new oil bonanzas to satisfy the growing demands of industrialization. Slick made an impact by aggressively seeking oil and gas throughout the Mid-Continent field. Many people in Oklahoma, Kansas, and Texas benefited from his enterprises. And even though he shared several characteristics with other oilmen of the day, his style, accomplishments, and good fortune made him a legend, somewhat apart from his peers. By general consensus of the press and the oil fraternity, Slick emerged as the largest independent producer of oil in the United States; he was regarded as the "King of the Wildcatters." Also significant was the role he played in the oil conservation movement in Oklahoma. He strongly advocated the use of unitization and proper well-spacing as means of efficiently and profitably producing oil. Slick experimented with these techniques and urged cooperation by oilmen in implementing these and other methods.

In completing this work I have incurred debts that mere acknowledgment can only begin to repay. I begin by thanking Arrell Morgan Gibson and John Ezell for encouraging me to pursue the writing of a biography of the elusive Tom Slick. A large measure of thanks goes to Norman Crockett, who read the draft and other versions of this manuscript. He has provided wise counsel throughout, and his criticism has been invaluable. I also extend my gratitude to Paul Glad, William T. Hagan, and H. Wayne Morgan for reading this work. Their thoughtful suggestions enabled me to make numerous improvements. A special measure of appreciation is extended to Charles Urschel "Chuck" Slick, whose interest in his grandfather's life made this project possible. I thank him for sharing his time, information, resources, and family connections. This project could not have been completed without his generous support.

I am also indebted to several other individuals and institutions for their assistance. Donald DeWitt and John Lovett of the Western History Collections, University of Oklahoma Library, accepted the business papers and photographs of Thomas B. Slick and established a collection in his name. Mr. Lovett was particularly helpful in providing copies of the photographs and for doing numerous favors. This work would have been more difficult without the assistance of Mary Moran and her staff in the Newspaper Division of the Oklahoma Historical Society. Much of the information on Slick was gleaned from hundreds of newspapers in this collection. I also wish to thank the staff of the Kansas Historical Society in Topeka for helping me to use my time wisely during my visit there. I am deeply grateful to John Caldwell of Louisiana Tech University for preparing the maps on such short notice and under such generous terms of credit. All of those who gave freely of their time to allow me to interview them receive my sincere thanks as well.

My deepest gratitude is reserved for my wife, my children, and my parents. Their unfailing support and total dedication have made most of my work possible. I am fortunate to have a wife whose great virtues are patience and understanding. Yet despite the guidance, assistance, and support of all those noted, errors no doubt remain, and for them I take full responsibility.

"King of the Wildcatters"

Introduction

"I DON'T LIKE PUBLICITY"

*Now, boys, you can say anything you want to about
the oil industry, my operations, my sale to the Prairie Oil and Gas or any other sales, but don't you
say anything personal about Tom Slick. I don't want
you to, and I won't stand for it—I'm not going to
tell you anything about him.*

Tom Slick to reporters

*Tom Slick's entrance into the oil business in the early 1900s came at a time of
incredible growth and change.* Leaving his home in Clarion, Pennsylvania, he
traveled to the emerging giant Mid-Continent oil field of Kansas and Oklahoma to pursue his career. At first he experienced only failure, but later he achieved
distinction as one of the largest individual oil producers in the nation. Despite
this notoriety, he shunned media attention and continued his work in the
manner that had brought him such great success. Although he was an enig-
matic figure, Slick's life reveals much about the times in which he lived and
about the conduct of the oil business from 1900 to 1930.

Tom Slick remained an independent oilman throughout his career, as did
many others. He made his own managerial decisions. He did not have stockholders to consider, nor did he have a powerful administrative staff with which

to contend. The label "independent" also meant that the operator engaged almost solely in exploration, drilling, and production. This type of oilman seldom entered the transporting, refining, or marketing of oil. As one writer noted, in Slick's oil business he was the "whole cheese."[1]

Slick never combined his holdings with any other oil company. He preferred to sell his oil properties when he grew tired of the work and then start over again, always as an independent. Indeed, many independents chose to follow this pattern because it provided quick profits with which they could finance explorations for oil in other areas. They also found it easier to sell out than to compete against the major firms that already had pipelines, refineries, and markets.

Slick's strong sense of independence may have stemmed, in part, from the fact that he grew up in an area of Pennsylvania where a local group of small, independent producers had boldly expressed their distaste for the major companies and the corporate combinations by declaring that "the small producers of Clarion County do hereby resolve that we, the said small producers, don't care a damn for the combination or for the large producers or for anybody else."[2] Later, young Slick arrived in Kansas at a time when independent oil producers were waging their fierce legislative and judicial battle against the monopoly of Standard Oil.

Slick, like many others, started with the financial backing of someone else. His first financial assistance came from a prominent Kansas City businessman; a Chicago oilman with ties to Pittsburgh banking backed him in his first successful oil well. However, Slick and other emerging independents asserted their financial and managerial independence as soon as possible. The new independents had to survive and compete against the established operators by reducing their operating costs to a minimum.

Getty Oil Company founder, J. Paul Getty, once noted that he and other small independents "concentrated on keeping our overhead expenses down. We sought our experts among the veteran oil field workers who formed our prospecting and drilling crews, or we relied on our own judgment and experience to solve our problems as they arose." Getty went on to say, "We did our own administrative and paper work and held both to absolute minimums. As for our offices, these were, more often than not, our mud-splotched automobiles or tiny, desk-space cubicles in some sagging building located in a low rent neighborhood."[3] Once they achieved a certain measure of success they might obtain new offices and hire additional staff, but they continued to operate their business as an individual enterprise. Slick was always characterized as an oilman who "worked out of his hip pocket." He remained in absolute control whether his office was located in his buckboard as at Cushing in 1912 or in his suite at the luxurious Colcord Building of Oklahoma City in the later 1920s.

Slick maintained this control even though his holdings could be found scattered in Oklahoma, Kansas, and Texas. Such personal control allowed Slick and other smaller independents to move quickly when they became aware of new oil prospects. Slick always seemed to obtain choice leases in prospective oil areas because he could visit the area, buy leases, make arrangements, and close deals before other firms could mobilize their forces of oil scouts, geologists, lease men, lawyers, accountants, drilling crews, and so forth. Stories abounded about how he negotiated drilling or lease deals over the telephone, at lunch, on a street corner, and many other places. Only in the last years of his life did he delegate any measure of authority or decision-making power to his subordinates. In 1929 he allowed his partners in Kansas, Ralph Pryor and Floyd Lockhart, to manage his business affairs with a considerable degree of autonomy. Even so he remained in contact with them by telephone. Also in 1929 he gave his associate, Ernest E. Kirkpatrick, a reasonably free hand in developing his Asher, Oklahoma, acreage.

Three different accounts describing seemingly typical days in Slick's office leave little doubt about his personal control over his business. On one occasion in 1927 Slick announced that he would be assembling a block of acreage in Logan County, Oklahoma. A newspaper reporter described how Slick dealt with the crowd of lease brokers that flocked to his office, noting that he spoke with each person in short, terse sentences that conveyed his businesslike and decisive style. "'What have you got?' he said to one broker. The man showed his plat. 'What's the price?' 'Five dollars.' 'I'll take it.' 'What have you?' he asked another. 'How much? Ten dollars? That's too high. My limit is $5 to $7 an acre. Can't use it unless you get the price down. Got about enough anyway. Who's next? No, don't want that at any price. Too far away. . . .' 'That's all today. I'm a busy man this afternoon. Come back in the morning.'"[4] Slick then disappeared into his private office.

In 1929 another reporter visited Slick's office, hoping to receive an interview with the oilman. As he waited in the lobby he observed lease brokers, geologists, and engineers walking nervously, holding blueprints, plat maps, and other business papers. All were watching the doors to Slick's office. Once inside, the reporter noted that Slick had a plat book of the Mid-Continent oil field on his desk and that during their visit the telephone rang numerous times:

> I [can't] recall how many times our talk was interrupted by the ringing of the telephone, which rested on the end of a movable bracket at his elbow. I don't know how many deals he made over the telephone in that hour and a half, but he did

make several, as I know by what he said. The bell would jingle, he would grab the telephone quickly, jerk it to him, talking all the time across his desk, and not until the receiver was at his ear would he stop one conversation and begin another: "Yes, I hear you, go on," a moment of tense listening, then, "No, thank you, I don't want that lease." Another time: "Yes—where is that lease?" and he leaned forward, the receiver to his ear, his forefinger tracing on the map in front of him, as he repeated the range, township and section numbers. "Yes, I know the tract, forty acres; you want $3,000 bonus; can you deliver a clear title to it? All right, bring in your papers and get your money." And slam, the receiver goes back to its place, he shoves the telephone away, turns and resumes the conversation where he left off.[5]

Clifford L. Frates, Slick's brother-in-law, recounted yet another hectic scene on one of his visits to his office. Frates said that when he arrived two men were trying to convince Slick to buy leases. At the same time Slick's tailor attempted to take the oilman's measurements. The ringing of the telephone added to the tension of the situation. At this point one of the men mentioned a gusher on acreage near his leases, and this captured Slick's undivided interest. Slick ordered the tailor to fit the suits for Frates and turned his attention to the potential oil deal.[6]

By 1930, few if any oilmen operated businesses of the magnitude of Slick's in this intense personal manner. In this regard Slick was perhaps more the exception than the rule for the period of his career from 1926 to 1930. At this time the nature of the oil business began to change. A historian, in an article aptly titled "The Passing of the Small Oil Man," noted that by 1930 most of the shallow pools of oil in the Mid-Continent field had been discovered. These pools had benefited the small producer since they could be drilled with relatively little capital. From 1900 to 1918 these shallow pools required wells from 400 to 2,500 feet deep with drilling costs ranging from $2.00 to $6.25 per foot. Thereafter, costs rose steadily owing to higher metal prices, deeper drilling, and other factors. In the 1920s, with many wells over 3,000 feet, the average price per foot had risen to about $17.00. These higher costs of drilling, in the Oklahoma City area, for example, forced many of the smaller operators out of business.[7] Even larger oil companies had to be more selective in their wildcatting ventures since drilling expenses on a deep, dry hole could be ruinous.[8] Slick managed to survive because he possessed both capital and ambition.

Slick typified oilmen of the day in another respect: he was only one of the many who followed the oil bonanzas as they moved westward from Pennsylvania and West Virginia. Slick, his father and brother, several of Slick's drillers, many of his business partners, as well as other men prominent in the oil industry, all hailed from eastern towns. One wag claimed that the Mid-Continent area had more Pennsylvanians than Pennsylvania.

As these eastern oilmen trekked westward, they brought their knowledge, experience, and biases to the emerging giant Mid-Continent area. For example, many of them arrived with a basic mistrust of formal geology. Most of them, by sheer experience, had a rudimentary understanding of "creekology," or judging a prospect by the lay of the land. But they came to the Mid-Continent in a period when geology was slowly becoming more acceptable and when geologists could claim success in locating oil. There were other signs of growing acceptance as well. From 1900 to 1930 universities established programs for petroleum geology; trade journals, such as the *Oil Weekly* and the *Oil and Gas Journal,* printed hundreds of articles on geology and its application to the oil industry; and many companies began hiring geologists.[9]

Although Slick played his "hunches" and drilled where he thought he would find oil, he too came to accept geology as an important aspect of the oil industry. In his early years he reportedly scoffed at geologists, but by the 1920s, he had apparently begun to change his views. He occasionally consulted geologists, though he sometimes ignored their advice. In 1923 he allowed the United States Bureau of Mines to construct a peg model in an office on his Endicott lease near Tonkawa, Oklahoma. This model depicted the contours of the geologic formations for that prolific oil area and was the first of its kind in an actively developing field in Oklahoma.[10] Several years later, during the Oklahoma City oil boom, Slick hired his first full-time geologist.[11]

The emerging conservation movement of the late 1920s was another aspect of the oil industry in which Slick acted in general accordance with other independents. Many oilmen feared that the proposed conservation techniques such as shutdown agreements, proration, well spacing, and unitization of pools would benefit the major corporations at the expense of the independents.[12] Their greatest concern, and the key idea expressed by Slick, was that whatever technique the operators and the state regulatory agencies agreed upon should be fairly applied. All operators, large and small, should benefit so that oil could be efficiently produced at the highest price.

A biographer of Ernest W. Marland, founder of Marland Oil Company, perceived a characteristic common to most oilmen—their passion for sport and gambling. He observed that "every species of animal that defends itself, or depends upon the overtaking or destruction of others for food, must spend much time playing. The play of such animals is utilitarian, since in it they re-enact the manner in which they defend themselves or the craft by which they take their prey. . . . Acquisitive men usually play those games wherein they seem to be keeping bright their power to remain in the struggle."[13] H. L. Hunt, professional gambler and later founder of Hunt Oil Company, once responded to a question about his occupation by saying, "By title, I guess I'd be considered a gambler, but I'm fixing to enter the oil business."[14] Thus Hunt's former occupation provided some measure of training for his new one.

Slick exhibited these same traits, perhaps to an exaggerated degree. He loved to gamble, whether it involved a block of acreage condemned by geologists or a game of cards.[15] One writer said of Slick, "He is said to play a wicked hand of poker and can talk the language that . . . dominoes like to hear. Cracks were made to pitch nickels, dimes, and quarters at, so he is said to believe, and there wouldn't be much fun sitting around a parlor listening to a radio when there's a bridge table handy."[16] Slick participated in outdoor sports as well. He liked tennis and golf but especially enjoyed hunting and fishing. Each fall (from 1925 to 1929) Slick treated his closest friends to an all-expense-paid hunting excursion to the Saint Charles Bay Hunting Club near Rockport, Texas. During these two-week trips they fished and hunted ducks, geese, and deer.[17] Slick also hunted on a preserve that he owned in Louisiana and on his plantations in Mississippi. On one or two occasions Slick took fishing trips to Canada.[18] It was clear, however, that he lacked the time to enjoy these pursuits as often as he would have liked.

Though Slick typified many wealthy oilmen of his day, he differed in some respects. He generally avoided conspicuous displays of wealth. Slick owned three relatively modest homes in Oklahoma City; Clarion, Pennsylvania; and San Antonio. He also purchased some furs and jewelry for his wife, and he maintained a chauffeur.[19] But the Slick children received their elementary education in the public school systems of Oklahoma City and San Antonio. He dressed in average attire. As one writer noted in a description of the oilman, "He had on low-cut tan shoes, a comfortable looking pair of shoes, wrinkled from long wear and worn a little at the heels. His clothing was black, his waistcoat was open and cigarette ashes were spilled all down its front and upon his coat lapels."[20]

His peers, like Lew Wentz, Frank Phillips, Ernest W. Marland, and others, were widely known for their philanthropy. Slick made no mention of his support for causes in charity or philanthropy. In fact, he once complained that "every time a story about me appears in the newspapers it seems that all the cranks and beggars in the country get busy. They flood me with letters, lie in wait for me, [and] make of themselves a great nuisance. They think I have millions to give away."[21] Yet despite these remarks he probably made some contributions. Several associates of Slick, who had knowledge of his financial affairs, noted at the time of the oilman's death, "He gave thousands of dollars to charity, of which no one will ever know, other than the beneficiaries. The extent of his philanthropy and donations to various charities are not generally known. He requested his closest business associates to make no mention and to give no publicity to such matters. He steadfastly refused to make any donation that would occasion publicity."[22] But secrecy in private affairs was a hallmark of Slick's character, and existing records failed to indicate charity to anyone other than family and friends.

He shared a great deal of his wealth with his family and friends. Slick provided generously for his family through his will. He routinely helped friends by backing them in business deals or with outright gifts of money. In one instance he paid for a friend's crippled son to receive orthopedic care at a Philadelphia hospital.[23] In another example, Slick wrote to a close friend and his wife, "I have tried to do a great many things to help my friends and it is so seldom that they really appreciate what you are doing for them. I feel that you and Harry really do appreciate the Endicott Lease [at Tonkawa] and that it will make life much pleasanter for you as it will give you a feeling of safety in case of sickness or death. I think this feeling means more than the things that money buys."[24] "He gives away a great deal, especially to old friends who have 'gone broke' in the oil game," a journalist wrote in 1929, "but never a cent to strangers."[25]

Another feature that set Slick apart from most of his peers was his abiding distaste for publicity or self-revelation of any sort. During a career that spanned nearly thirty years he gave only one formal interview, and this only after warning the reporter, "I don't like publicity. . . . I've never given out an interview. In all my life I've never talked for publication. A big magazine sent a man here the other day, all the way from New York, and I wouldn't see him. I don't like to talk through the newspapers and magazines."[26] Slick also left very few personal papers, only a few letters and two speeches.

However, people's actions can provide insights into their personalities. In view of this, it seems Slick possessed three main characteristics: first, and foremost, he was a driven man in terms of his work; second, he had a deep devotion to family and friends; and third, he had great pride in his reputation.

That Slick thrived on his work cannot be questioned. His career centered on the fact that he would work strenuously to build up a vast amount of oil production, then sell his holdings and start over. To all who met him, Slick seemed to be a bundle of nervous energy. The journalist who interviewed Slick in 1929 commented on his nervous habits: "I cannot tell how many cigarettes Mr. Slick smoked in the hour and a half I was with him. . . . Every few minutes he would lift the package, dig out a cigarette, light it and consume it in four or five long, deep drags." He continued, "Nor can I tell how many times, as we talked, he got up and walked quickly across the room as if he were starting for somewhere—just a nervous urge to be moving that projected his tall, gaunt figure out of its chair, across the room in quick strides, wheeling there to return and drop into the chair again, his long, shapely fingers reaching for another cigarette."[27] Work released his energy. He was in full and constant control of his business, and he generally failed to balance his strenuous work life with an appropriate amount of leisure and recreation.

Slick had a deep devotion to his family and friends. For his parents and his sister he had a genuine attachment. The loss of his father in 1912 came as a severe blow and, coupled with other stressful events in his life, contributed to his nervous and physical breakdown several months later. Slick traveled often, especially in his younger years, to Clarion to visit his mother and sister. He saw his sister more frequently after she married his best friend, Charles Urschel, and the couple moved to Oklahoma. Slick displayed a deep attachment to his wife and children as well. The family spent time each summer in Clarion, each winter in San Antonio. A friend of the family remembered that Slick would take his children for walks in the woods near their home in Clarion and that he enjoyed romping in the yard with them. But, thriving on his work as he did, he probably did not spend as much time with his family as they would have liked. A family friend related that Slick once went upstairs to tell his children good night and that he would be leaving Clarion to return to Oklahoma and check on some of his wells. His oldest son told him that sometimes he wished that his father did not have any oil wells. Slick agreed.[28]

Slick felt justifiable pride in his reputation as a fair and honest person. He went to great lengths to obviate anything that might impinge upon his reputation. He once stated that everyone "knows that Tom Slick never tells a lie. When I tell a man I'll do so and so I'll do it if I have to tear the shirt off my back. . . . I play fair with the farmers I lease from. When I sell my oil the landowner gets all that's coming to him."[29] He apparently dealt fairly with everyone, including the blacks who owned land near Langston, Oklahoma. One story of the day related how Langston had a sign at its outskirts that read, "All whites should leave this town by sundown." When Slick became interested in the oil possibilities on the southeast edge of town he sent his chauffeur (who was black) as an emissary. As a relative of Slick's told the story, "He sent Jewel [his chauffeur] . . . up to Langston to buy leases and equipped him with plenty of strawberry soda pop and they had barbecues and what not and signed up a number of leases for which he paid the blacks the going price. The sign was then changed to read, 'All whites should leave this town by sundown, except Tom Slick.'"[30] He had begun the cultivation of his reputation many years before at a place less than twenty miles from Langston, near the tiny community of Tryon, Oklahoma. It was there that Slick embarked upon a career that would lead from a dismal record of ten straight dry holes and the nickname of "Dry Hole Slick" to his acclaim as the greatest independent oil producer in the United States.

His entrance into the oil business just after 1900 came at a time when the industry stood on the threshold of becoming an economic giant. From 1859 to 1900 oil had been used primarily for illumination and lubrication. The early fields of Pennsylvania, West Virginia, and Indiana had been able to meet this limited demand. After 1900, oil entered what one historian termed "the Age of Energy." The invention of the automobile and the conversion of other modes of transportation from coal to petroleum-based fuels guaranteed the rise of this industry to prominence. As demand skyrocketed, oilmen expanded their search for new supplies to keep pace. Indeed, one of the industry's key problems in 1900 was finding new reserves of oil.[31] It was to this task that Slick and others set themselves as they headed west.

"I'm a Born Trader"

There is a legend in the oil fields that some men are approached early in life by a bird made of cast iron, whose voice is found in the hoarse squawk of a walking beam in need of oil, in the shriek of a wild plume of black oil tearing from the ground into the freedom of the sky, and in the hissing roar of a wild gas fire, lighting up the earth like a tremendous red torch. Once a man has been visited by the Dicky Bird, he will never find rest until he has cast all else aside and plunged into the feverish search for oil, wherever it might lead him.

Bob Duncan,
The Dicky Bird Was Singing

Thomas B. Slick seemed destined to be an oilman. Some people, based on the circumstances of their birth and their upbringing, are well suited to engage in certain types of employment. Environment and family connections can have some degree of impact on job choice. Slick once remarked, "I came west from Clarion, Pa., where I was born among the oil derricks. The first sniff of air I ever breathed into my nostrils was laden with the odor of oil."[1] Perhaps his birth near the origin of America's oil industry, where he came into contact with the sights, sounds, and smells of oil wells, attracted him. It might have been the allure of wealth, the hope of adventure, or the "call of the Dicky Bird."

Slick could only trace his antecedents as far as his grandfathers on both sides of his family. His paternal grandfather, Alfred J. L. Slick was born in February 1811, probably in western Pennsylvania and possibly to a family that had moved from Maryland. The family was of Dutch or German heritage. Sometime between 1850 and 1860 Alfred Slick, a tailor by trade, moved to Clarion, Pennsylvania, and married. To this union four children were born.

Alfred Slick served three years with the 11th Pennsylvania Cavalry during the American Civil War. By 1870, census records revealed that he lived alone; either his wife, Margaret, had died or they no longer lived together. It was sometime around 1870 that one of his sons, Johnson M. Slick, left home. Alfred lived until 1901, when he died in Clarion at the age of ninety.[2]

Thomas Baker, Tom Slick's maternal grandfather, came to the United States from England in 1843 or 1844. He and his wife settled at Shippenville, Pennsylvania, only five miles northwest of Clarion. There the couple established and operated the first commercial flour mill in the town.[3] The Shippenville miller and his wife had eight children. One daughter, Amanda, married William Reardon, and the couple moved only four miles from her parents and established their own flour mill at Knox, Pennsylvania. The youngest daughter, Mary A. Baker, occasionally visited her older sister Amanda, and this was probably where she met her future husband.

When the fourteen-year-old Johnson M. Slick left his father's home around 1870 he made his way to Knox and began working in William and Amanda Reardon's flour mill. He lived with them at first, but after a few years he most likely lived on his own. Sometime between 1870 and 1880 Johnson met Mary Baker, and, as the family story has been passed down, "he mixed a little love with his flour."[4] In 1880 Johnson M. Slick and Mary A. Baker married. He was twenty-four years old, and she twenty. The newlyweds then moved to Shippenville, where Johnson gained employment at his new father-in-law's mill. Later that same year Mary gave birth to their first child, Jesse Guy Slick. Three years later, on October 12, 1883, their second son was born, and they named him for her father, Thomas Baker Slick. Flored Mae, the last of their children, arrived five years later in 1888.[5] In 1892 the Slick family moved to Clarion where Johnson bought his own flour mill.[6]

At about this same time Johnson Slick entered the oil business, eventually becoming a contract driller. This meant that he probably owned his own drilling rig and contracted his services to drill wells for others. Or he could have offered his talents to those who already owned a rig. In either case he began work as a driller and operated in western Pennsylvania. This area had proven to be quite productive since Edwin Drake's discovery of oil near Titusville in

1859. The discovery well was only about twenty-five miles from Shippenville. This new industry offered ready employment to those with plenty of physical stamina. It also was alluring as a source of great wealth. Johnson's reasons for engaging in the oil business were not recorded, but his decision to do so surely had an impact on his two sons.

Extant records revealed little regarding the childhood and adolescent years of Tom Slick. He most likely attended the public schools of Shippenville and Clarion. One journalist recorded that Tom "grew into a sturdy young [man] just like other boys in the community. He hunted, fished and played. . . . He helped his father in the flour mill and his mother and the family by taking his part in the home."[7] After high school, Slick received no further formal education. A friend said that when Slick was sixteen years old, in 1899, he went to West Virginia to visit his father and his brother who were working on an oil rig there.[8] If true, this probably had a great impact on the young Slick. But he returned to Clarion, and the 1900 census still listed him as a student. His father and brother appeared on the rolls as oil field workers.[9]

The influences on Tom Slick to enter the oil business were readily apparent, his father and brother being the most obvious. Johnson's area of drilling interests had expanded quickly and by 1894 included new developments in West Virginia, Kentucky, and Virginia.[10] Several of Tom Slick's relatives on the Baker side of the family engaged in the oil business as well. Lot G. Baker and A. P. Baker were both lease men in Clarion and Butler Counties of Pennsylvania. Lawrence A. Baker served as a gauger for Standard Oil in the Shippenville area, while another cousin, Thomas W. Baker, also of Shippenville, worked as a drilling contractor in western Pennsylvania and Ohio.[11] Slick likely had friends and neighbors also involved in oil.

Slick's residence "among the oil derricks," as he phrased it, must have had an impact as well. Oil drilling activity in western Pennsylvania centered on the tri-county area of Venango, Butler, and Clarion Counties. Various oil booms had emerged in this region in the decades of the 1860s through the 1890s. During the years of Slick's childhood, drilling activity commenced with the opening of the Clarion pool in 1887 and continued for the next two years. In 1889 there was even a minor oil boom in his hometown of Shippenville.[12] (It was about this time that his father became interested in oil.) Then after the family moved to Clarion a slight resurgence in drilling began around that town. At least fifteen rigs were operating in 1896 on the east side of Clarion where the Slick family lived.[13] With these drilling operations only a few blocks from his home, Tom Slick possibly watched the progress on these wells, especially since his father and brother were by then drillers in West Virginia and Kentucky.

Meanwhile, the drilling activity spread westward. Oil fields opened in Ohio, Indiana, Kentucky, Illinois, Kansas, and Indian Territory. The great gusher at Spindletop, Texas, in 1901 heralded the emergence of a new oil region there, but it was the oil fields being opened in Kansas in 1903 that lured Johnson Slick and his sons from Pennsylvania.[14]

The trio arrived at Chanute, Kansas, in June 1903. Here Slick's father and brother operated an oil rig for a newcomer to the oil industry, Alexander Massey. In 1902 Massey sold his business, the Massey Iron Company of Kansas City, and invested all of his money in oil.[15] Massey and two associates formed the Spurlock Petroleum Company in December 1902 to develop a large tract of acreage near Peru, Kansas. With an amazing record of success, the company struck oil or gas with its first twenty-five wells. Production came from shallow sands and was quite small, generally fifty barrels or less per day for each well.[16]

Massey's achievements were part of the rapid development of the area. Within six months he and the same associates formed another company to develop property adjacent to that drilled by Spurlock. The White Sand Oil Company began drilling in June 1903, and it too enjoyed early success. Seven of nine wells were producers, with a total production of three hundred barrels of crude oil daily. Within another six months Massey and his partners formed a new company, which experienced equal good fortune. Their Central Pool Oil Company got production from its first six wells.[17] Massey's phenomenal success no doubt stirred the young Tom Slick and kindled in him a desire to enter the oil business.

On June 5, 1903, one Chanute newspaper noticed the arrival in Kansas of three men from Pennsylvania, "J. M. Slick, with his two sons, Jesse and T. B. from Clarion, Pa., have just reached our city, and will engage in oil drilling. Mr. Slick has had much experience in oil operations. . . . The older [son] will engage with Mr. Slick in the oil business."[18] Johnson Slick was the driller, and Jesse worked as his assistant. Tom, however, went to work as a salesman for the Oil Well Supply Company in Chanute. After several months at this job Tom Slick resigned and went to Peru, Kansas, to join his father and brother.[19] Massey commented that one day in early 1904 he visited the rig and noticed a new young man. "He was slim and wiry, light-haired. He was dressed about as simply as any son of an itinerant driller staking his last penny on each hole could be. Tom was hauling water for his dad, doing odd jobs, anything to try and earn his keep." After several weeks' work and no apparent self-fulfillment from hauling water, the frustrated Tom asked, "Can't you get me a real job, Mr. Massey?"[20]

To date Slick had not had "a real job" in the oil business, although many

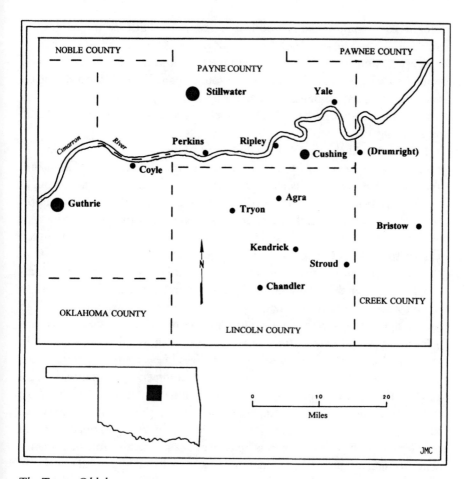

The Tryon, Oklahoma, area

years later the legend would contend that he had done everything. One account noted that young Tom began his oil field experience "by thoroughly training himself in all the work connected with developments in oil and gas. No part of the mechanical work connected therewith was neglected or evaded; he went through it all until every operation was fully understood and the knowledge how to do them was at his command."[21] Still other versions stated that he had worked as a "roustabout" and as a cable tool dresser. But Slick later dispelled these myths, declaring, "I never drove a mule in my life, nor dressed a drill. I would have done those things if I had to, but I just didn't."[22]

Rather than do this type of work, Slick proposed to Massey that he would make a good leaser. Johnson Slick agreed reluctantly that his son made up with persistence what he lacked in experience. When Massey asked Slick if he thought Tom would make a good leaser, he replied that even though his son had never made a lease, "I believe he's got the stuff for one. . . . If you notice, he never lets go when he starts anything."[23] For whatever reason, Massey decided to take a chance on the eager young man. Tom Slick no doubt responded with great excitement when in August 1904 Massey said, "Well, Tom let's you and me go down in Oklahoma, eat some mushrooms and maybe do some leasing."[24]

Massey and Slick selected Lincoln County, Oklahoma, as a likely place to prospect for oil—nearly forty miles from the nearest oil activity at Cleveland, Oklahoma. He outfitted his lease man with new shoes and clothes, a buckboard, and a two-horse team to give him a look of respectability. More important for Slick's career was the fact that Massey agreed to give him a 25 percent share in all leases taken.[25] Thus, failure (or success) could come, but at limited expense to Slick, as Massey bore most of the costs.

Leasing practices in the Mid-Continent area followed a fairly uniform pattern then and for the remainder of Slick's career. After choosing the area in which to drill, the lease man visited the surrounding landowners and asked them to sign. The two parties would negotiate terms, generally similar to these: 1) the lease would extend for five years or as long as oil was produced in commercial quantities; 2) the oil company would begin drilling within one year of signing the lease; 3) if they failed to commence drilling within the specified time, they would pay the landowner a "rental fee," the standard amount being one dollar per acre, but, depending on the potential of the area, the price might range from ten cents to several hundred dollars per acre; 4) some leases provided for a "bonus" payment as an incentive for the property owner to sign, a figure that varied widely, ranging from the typical one dollar to thousands of dollars; and 5) the landowner retained one-eighth of the royalties on any oil and gas produced, while the oil company received the remainder.[26]

Tom Slick arrived at Tryon, Oklahoma, in late August 1904. The town newspaper noted that Slick would be taking leases and that his firm would "sink a well inside of one year."[27] After two weeks of limited success Slick had been able to convince only a few of the area farmers to sign leases. At this point Slick returned to Kansas to confer with Massey on what could be done. Massey agreed to return to Tryon with Slick to try and persuade the townspeople of his sincerity of drilling for oil. Massey hoped that media pressure might induce the hesitant farmers to sign up, and for the next several weeks local boosters printed articles in the *Tryon News* encouraging them to sign.[28] In addition, the Kansas oilman informed the town leaders that he wanted their cooperation in helping him and Slick to assemble a large block of acreage *before* he would start drilling. Otherwise, he would not drill for oil.[29] If the two men were fortunate enough to find oil, controlling most of the acreage around the proposed well would give them a commanding advantage over any competition that might emerge. Meanwhile, Slick continued to search the countryside for new leases, and the newspaper assured farmers that they had nothing to lose by signing a lease. He used his friendly manner as a means of persuasion, and he even joined the local Masonic Lodge No. 96 as a sign of his desire to be accepted as a member of the community.[30] However, few additional leases were signed. Massey, true to his word, took Slick, and they departed by train for Kansas City on November 22, 1904.

That week the *Tryon News* published a scathing article critical of the reluctant farmers, asking, "Where is the fellow that thought they were bluffing about going away if they did not get these leases arranged? Don't you fellows that were so distressingly contrary in this matter feel a little like kicking yourselves by allowing such a good opportunity . . . to pass, possibly . . . for years?"[31] The writer assured the readers that this deal could bring them financial independence and would benefit the entire community as well. "Have you oil under your land; if so why not get it on the market? It is no value to you 2000 feet under ground. If you desire to get it up to the surface and on the market, when and how are you going to do it? . . . The large bulk of notes in the banks and mortgages of record in the county," the editorial reminded the reluctant ones, "is conclusive proof that the farmers will never be in a position to delve into the earth after oil. Why do you not get this oil on the market and relieve yourselves of these burdensome obligations and change your bank account from debit to credit?" The writer pointed out that in addition to the lease money the farmer would benefit from higher property values and that the oil industry would create a market for his produce. "Now all you people that have the welfare of the country in general at heart, get to work and arrange these differences and get Mr. Massey back here so work may begin at once; and this decision will be the beginning of a plan that will relieve the farmers of this country of their fast increasing indebtedness that is a cloud in their pathway, a blight on their homes and a continual menacing obstacle in the highway of progress."[32]

Massey did not make the citizens of Tryon regret their obstinacy for long: the following week the newspaper gleefully reported that Tom Slick was back in town taking leases again. By mid-December Massey's threat of withdrawal from the project had the desired effect, as Slick finally obtained all of the required leases by that time.[33] Massey and Slick proceeded at once to uphold their part of the bargain. On January 6, 1905, the newspaper reported that workers had completed the derrick on the M. C. Teegarden farm and that the drilling machinery would soon arrive. Next, Slick secured the services of drilling contractors C. C. Hubbard and W. F. McCoy, both of Chanute, Kansas.[34] With all arrangements completed, the drillers waited for a break in the intense winter weather so that they could proceed.

Drilling began on Wednesday, January 18, 1905, and progressed slowly during the next two months. Cold weather, losing the drill bit, and drilling into water caused routine delays, yet Slick, Massey, and the people of Tryon remained optimistic. Massey affirmed his confidence in the area by building a warehouse and office in Tryon in February of 1905, which served as the headquarters for Massey Oil Company. The office was a two-story, neatly painted building measuring sixteen by thirty feet. Slick and Massey lived on the second story, with office and storage space on the first floor. Massey apparently looked upon Slick with great affection. John Bennington, a Tryon town leader and businessman, observed, "The building in Tryon, nice in its arrangement, was much more for the enjoyment of Mr. Slick than anyone else. [Mr. Massey looked after Slick] just like a solicitous father would look after a son."[35]

Meanwhile, Slick continued to take leases, soon acquiring a total of twenty-seven thousand acres. He apparently took Massey's advice that a good lease should be "one unencumbered by special clauses or provisos, but as simple as possible." As Massey recalled many years later, Slick "was a whiz, Tom would go out and lease most of a territory as yet unproved or doubtful as to oil prospects. But he'd spread as clean a bunch of leases before a capitalist as you'd wish to see. . . . He certainly knew what a good oil lease was. Often as not the capitalist would buy the leases for that very reason. They were too clean to pass up."[36] Simple and honest leasing techniques served Slick well, as his future in the oil business proved.

As the Tryon drilling rig pounded deeper, other oil men grew more interested in the activities of Massey and Slick. Confident that the Tryon well would strike oil, they formulated plans to connect the Tryon area with the Cleveland area. Several drilling ventures began, generally along a line connecting the two towns. These new operations spread southwest toward Tryon, starting first at Yale in Payne County. As early as March 1905 the Sater Oil and Gas Company began drilling near Yale.[37] The next activity came near Ripley (about thirteen miles southwest of Yale or ten miles northeast of Tryon) when the soon-to-be-famous tandem of Michael L. Benedum and Joseph C. Trees started drilling a well near the town.[38] Their well showed only traces of oil and gas, but this was enough to encourage others that the entire area might prove to be an extension of the Cleveland field. Further southwest, at Perkins (only eight miles north of Tryon) the Kansas City firm Coffin-Halpin-Brady Oil and Development Company commenced the next test. The owners of this company notified the Perkins newspaper, "We are well pleased with the location of the land adjacent to Perkins as being in the oil belt and we have for sometime endeavored to get sufficient land in that vicinity to permit operation."[39] By July 1905 the company began drilling.

The new and exciting oil prospects generated numerous rumors about the possibilities for the future. Each town had its leaders who hoped the area would become the next Spindletop. Reporters visited the wells regularly to glean whatever morsel of information that could be obtained. Rumors and gossip abounded and often supplemented the truth about the wells. Or reporters simply exaggerated the facts. Such was the case with the Yale well in March 1905; newspapers reported that the well came in as a gusher. Tom Slick immediately went to visit the well and learned that the story was totally untrue.[40] He feared such reckless rumors because they often only served to drive up lease prices. They also inspired distrust and disillusionment if proven false. When Slick voiced his objections to this sort of journalism, an editorial in the *Tryon News* reminded him that he should tend to his oil well and that the reporters would take care of the news.[41]

Nevertheless, Massey and Slick triggered a minor boom in the Tryon vicinity. All area businesses experienced increased sales in lumber, building materials, and other supplies and services. The exhortations of the Tryon newspaper that all stood to benefit from the drilling activity seemed to be validated.[42] The editor believed that Slick deserved credit for his persistence in obtaining the leases and launching the oil boom. An article in the newspaper posed a rhetorical question for all those who doubted the intentions of Slick: "Don't you think it the right move . . . to apologize to 'Tom' and take off our hats in reverential manner to him for his indomitable services for our good?"[43] But to do so may have been premature, for at the well things were not proceeding as hoped.

In late June 1905 the drillers "shot" the well with a charge of nitroglycerin in an effort to fracture the formation so that oil could flow more freely. This action failed, however, and drilling continued. But after several more months Massey ran out of patience and was unwilling to continue spending money on what appeared to be a dry hole. So, at a depth of 2,800 feet, Slick's first drilling venture proved to be what was known as a "duster."[44]

Shortly after their failure at Tryon the two men terminated their partnership. Massey undoubtedly had spent far more money on the venture than he might otherwise have done. He was disappointed that this expensive effort was not as successful and profitable as his Kansas operations. Neither Massey nor Slick ever gave details on their separation. Massey would only say that he held no hard feelings toward Slick, it was simply "a case of a Scotchman . . . saying once is enough to a Pennsylvania Dutch boy."[45]

After this failure, Slick made another attempt at finding oil in Lincoln County at Kendrick, Oklahoma, about eleven miles southeast of Tryon. He probably drilled this well using his own money. The Kendrick newspaper indicated that Slick had selected a site on the John Seaba farm near town, and drilling commenced when the last holdout farmers signed their leases. Slick lived in the hotel at Kendrick while the well was being drilled in August 1906.[46] Months later, and with a second dry hole to his credit, Slick left Oklahoma.

Sometime early in 1907 Slick went to seek his fortune in the oil boom near Robinson, Illinois. His father and brother had already left the area. In 1905 Johnson and Jesse had separated; Johnson went to work in the oil and gas fields near Medicine Hat, Alberta, Canada, and Jesse returned to West Virginia.[47] Later in that same year Johnson Slick retired from the oil business and returned to Clarion. He resumed his former trade, using some of his oil earnings to build his own flour mill.[48]

But Tom left continuing to believe that he could find oil in Oklahoma if only he had the financial support to drill thorough tests. He set for himself the goal of becoming a millionaire. Many years later he told a reporter that in 1907 he decided that he would eventually go into the oil business on his own "and be a millionaire." When the reporter asked him if he deliberately set out to achieve this goal the oilman replied, "I did that, exactly. . . . My intention, right then, was to stick at it until I accumulated a million dollars."[49] After all, in November 1905 the Glenn Pool south of Tulsa emerged as a tremendous oil field, making several millionaires in the process. In Illinois Slick hoped to find the financial backing that would enable him to discover his own oil field. Slick did not know for years just how close he had been to discovering oil at Tryon when he stopped drilling at 2,800 feet. His intuition was correct, but he failed to drill deep enough. At 4,000 feet oil awaited those who possessed the money and daring to drill.

"Every Time I Drill a Well I Have to Get Another Partner"

*No man who has never had the experience can
understand the feeling of exhilaration that comes
when you bring in an oil well, especially your first
one. . . . There are no words to describe it. . . . You
are staggered and filled with awe at the realization
that you have triumphed over a stubborn and un-
yielding Nature, forcing her to give up some of
her treasure.*

Mike Benedum

*On March 17, 1987, an Oklahoma oil well achieved a unique distinction by
having a special United States Postal Service cancellation issued in honor of
the seventy-fifth anniversary of its discovery.* A rather commonplace brass
plaque also commemorates this well drilled at SWc NW NW Sec. 32-T18N-
R7E in Creek County:

> Site of the No. 1 F.M. Wheeler, discovery well of the Drumright-Cushing Oil Field.
> Its completion by C. B. Shaffer, et al., on April 1, 1912, set off one of the greatest
> 'oil booms' in history. The well produced oil for more than 35 years.[1]

One of those included in the "et al." of the inscription was the man responsible for selecting the site and for drilling the well, Tom Slick. This strike with the Wheeler well marked Slick's successful entrance into the oil business, it launched the development of the Cushing Field, and it provided the basis of many individual fortunes.

Five years of relative obscurity preceded the years for which Slick was best known. After the failure of the Tryon and Kendrick wells, he departed for Illinois. Here, a well-known oilman, Charles B. Shaffer of Pittsburgh, hired Slick to obtain leases at a salary of one hundred dollars per month, plus expenses. Shaffer had already become a millionaire in the oil fields of western Pennsylvania and had moved west, like so many others, in search of new oil bonanzas. The Shaffer and Smathers Company, based in Chicago, began searching for oil in Illinois in 1906, with their new employee obtaining leases there. Slick also prospected for the company in Kentucky and western Canada.[2] He soon convinced his employer that oil could be found in Oklahoma and that perhaps they should obtain some leases in that territory.

Slick returned to Creek County on behalf of Shaffer in early 1907. Shaffer planned to start near Sapulpa, then drill a well about every four miles and continue westward until he discovered oil.[3] Slick would move in advance and obtain the necessary acreage "with the understanding that he would be carried for an interest in all leases which he obtained under a certain sum per acre."[4] Court clerks recorded Slick's first lease in the area on December 7, 1907, and for the next seven years his name appeared scattered in the lease register.[5] Shaffer, however, lost interest and abandoned the drilling campaign after a series of failures.

Meanwhile, Slick decided to drill on some of his own acreage, which he had accumulated by using his wits. Mrs. E. F. Kelley, whose mother operated a boardinghouse where Tom Slick stayed occasionally, commented on how he was the "smartest thing you ever saw." She stated that he would buy leases in an area but would skip over some of them. "Later when he got the money he went back and bought that for himself."[6] In a 1951 interview, Tom Slick, Jr., said his father often convinced farmers to sign leases without a bonus payment. He assured them that they would make plenty of money in royalties when he struck oil. Slick would then drill a test well with his own money or with other financial backing.[7]

In the years from 1907 to 1911, while leasing for Shaffer in Oklahoma, Slick probably drilled as many as ten dry holes on his and Shaffer's leases.[8] The first of these came in January 1907 when the Bristow newspaper reported that "Mr. Slick was induced to come here by Messrs. [Cramer] & Longfellow" to drill a well five miles east of town. Slick used a portable "star rig" and drilled to a depth of 2,561 feet with good signs of oil and gas. By

June, Slick apparently ran out of money, so Bristow citizens made contributions to pay for 120 quarts of nitroglycerin to shoot the well. The shot failed to produce the desired effect, however, and caved in most of the well.[9]

For the next several months Slick frequently moved in and out of Oklahoma, usually making "business trips" to the East. One such trip was a ten-month excursion to Indiana, where Slick gathered leases, presumably for Shaffer, in the Oakland City area. On another 1909 trip Slick drilled a dry hole north of Catlettsburg in Boyd County, Kentucky. He received financial support for this failed venture from a Pittsburgh businessman.[10] Slick then spent much of 1910 in Canada obtaining leases for Shaffer. By early 1911 he began yet another drilling venture, this time near Mannford, in extreme northern Creek County. This well went down on land owned by Slick, Frank Barnes, Claude Freeland, and B. B. Jones, while Shaffer and Smathers provided some of the financial backing. The *Bristow Record* observed that Slick had moved to Tulsa while drilling the Mannford well but that in that area, "most of 'em are dry holes, so far."[11] This one was no exception when in June the casing collapsed and ruined the well.

Even before they abandoned the Mannford well, Shaffer and Slick tried again near Olive. The well, about one mile north of Olive, drew this comment from the Bristow newspaper: Slick "continues to gamble on wild cat stuff. Few men have stuck to the wild-catting longer and harder than Slick and associates. It is said he has spent $150,000 mostly on dry holes."[12] Despite these failures Shaffer retained Slick as an employee, although the exact terms of his employment remained vague. He continued to write a few leases, and their association endured because of the leases in which they shared interests. Slick, still convinced of the oil possibilities of Creek County, teamed with a prosperous Bristow businessman, B. B. Jones, who agreed to help him continue prospecting for oil.

Bernard B. Jones and his brother Montfort owned the Bank of Bristow, and both were early explorers for oil in Creek County.[13] Slick and B. B. Jones met, possibly as early as 1907 at the time of Slick's first lease near Bristow, and formed a friendship that lasted many years. Jones played a significant role in Slick's future: he introduced him to the woman that would become his wife, he served as the namesake for his eldest son, and, more immediately, he became his business partner. Jones and Slick agreed to drill their combined acreage in Creek County: Jones provided the financing and several leases while Slick drilled the wells and supplied additional leases.

Another associate, Charles J. Wrightsman (who might be called a "silent partner"), held a law degree from Georgetown University and had served as a member of the Oklahoma Territorial Legislature. Wrightsman practiced law in Tulsa after 1906 but spent much of his time in the oil business.[14] He furnished money to fund some of the efforts of Slick and Jones. Wrightsman also held an interest in many of the leases these two men drilled. The three men later formalized their association and created a lease-holding syndicate known as the Hi-Grade Oil Company.[15]

The new partners selected the Mamie Blackwell farm at NE NW 28-18-7 to begin their joint drilling venture in October 1911. The farm, located about thirteen miles east of Cushing and six miles southwest of Olive, was labeled by the newspapers as "pure wildcat territory."[16] As the well progressed it generated a fair amount of interest among oilmen, especially when in mid-November a Tulsa newspaper published an exaggerated report that the well began producing four hundred barrels per day.[17] Subsequent reports had the well producing only a small amount of oil from the shallow Layton sand, although the drilling was continuing.[18] One reporter observed that the Jones and Slick well was "better than is generally supposed and that if the well had been finished in that sand [Layton] it would have been a good producer."[19] Despite the small production the drillers continued until December 7, 1911. With only slight additional showings of oil they abandoned the well at a depth of 3,015 feet, but the favorable signs were incentive to begin two other tests.[20] The second test, one mile west (in section twenty-nine) had begun even before the Blackwell test had been abandoned. The other test was just north of the first two (in section twenty) on a lease shared with Shaffer.[21] Both tests had the same disappointing results—slight signs of oil but not enough for commercial production.[22]

But these signs whetted Tom Slick's appetite for more. He was sure that his next well would be a gusher. B. B. Jones, however, proved unwilling to fund another dry hole even though the well that Slick proposed to drill was on a lease owned by Jones. Jones wanted to continue drilling but with someone else's money. Needing funds to continue his drilling operations, Slick met with the Cushing Commercial Club and offered them half interest in all of his holdings if they would loan him eight thousand dollars to pay the drilling expenses for one more well.[23] "Local capitalists" in Cushing had made attempts in the past to locate oil near their town. In 1901–1902 (after the Red Fork discovery) investors had pooled their money to drill a well on the eastern edge of town. At a depth of nine hundred feet, after continual problems, they abandoned it. Again in 1906 (after the Glenn Pool discovery) Cushing investors made another attempt, this time west of town. The drillers faced the same problems as before and stopped the test at a depth of 1,100 feet.[24] Those experiences, along with Slick's recent string of failures, made the Commercial Club wary, and they refused his offer.

In the winter of 1911 Tom Slick reached the nadir of a career in oil that had barely begun. As one newspaper writer of the day quipped, Slick "was broke 'flat as a pancake.' . . . He could toss up a dollar, and it would change into ten cents before it hit the floor."[25] Contemporaries noted that Slick now considered himself a failure: "He had even asked Bristow friends . . . about some kind of employment where a man could make a dependable livelihood."[26] Another story related that in the winter of 1911, with temperatures dropping to the zero mark, Slick found his credit at the same level. Even so, he convinced a store owner to order a coat for him to be paid C.O.D. When the coat arrived and Slick could not pay for it, "the sympathetic merchant finally let him check it out during a cold spell and return it later."[27] This story illustrated perfectly a feature of the wildcatter's mentality—his obsession with finding oil. As one observer wrote, "When a man is exploring for oil, the only reality is the next wildcat, the one that will come in. He lives so completely in his undiscovered wealth that the struggle to pay his bills is what seems like a dream."[28]

At this point Slick turned to his former employer, Charles B. Shaffer. He borrowed a hundred dollars, probably from Jones, and went to Chicago to discuss his plans with Shaffer. Based on the oil and gas signs in the three test wells, and Slick's agreement to give Shaffer rights to some of his leases, Shaffer granted the eight-thousand-dollar loan.[29] The Chicago oilman trusted Slick and, no doubt, had confidence in the Creek County area as a potential oil field.

When Slick returned to Oklahoma he and his old partner B. B. Jones began selecting drilling sites in the Drumright area. (Drumright did not exist as a town until after the oil boom began. The area was generally known as the Tiger neighborhood.) His first and most significant selection was on the Frank M. Wheeler farm just north of Drumright.[30] Tradition had it that Slick visited the poor stonemason one winter night in December of 1911 and pleaded with him to lease his land. According to this version, Wheeler finally consented so that he could get rid of his pesky visitor and, lease in hand, Slick drove away in his buckboard the next morning.[31] But a Drumright historian recently discovered the inaccuracy of this account. Slick did call on Wheeler in late December 1911, but it could not have been to obtain a lease. According to Creek County court records, B. B. Jones had held the lease on the Wheeler farm since December 27, 1910. The records further revealed that Wheeler never leased any land to Tom Slick.[32] Thus the purpose of the visit was to inform Wheeler of their intention to drill and to select a site for the well.

Shaffer hoped to obtain a few leases in the surrounding area, just in case

Slick's luck improved. A Cushing newspaper gave the standard advice given by community boosters when oil prospectors came to the area: "Land owners have everything to gain and no risk to themselves in making leases. It costs from $8000 to $10,000 to put down a single hole. Unless the promoters can get the leases they want they will not chance their money here, while other localities are eager to give leases and even bonuses in money to get prospecting done."[33] A week later the other Cushing newspaper encouraged citizens to cooperate and furnish leases to Shaffer and Slick. It declared that these men were real developers and not just speculators. All who hindered their efforts hurt their own chances for material progress and those of the community. "Why close the door? . . . Why not help yourself? . . . And see what you stand to win, and run no risk. Mr. Slick takes the risk. . . . We would repeat that we believe it to [be in] the best interests of the individuals and all that these leases be granted. . . . And just a word of warning. If you make a lease see that the lessees name is not left blank, but that the name of Thomas B. Slick is there."[34]

Meanwhile, between January 22 and 25, 1912, Slick's contract drillers, David H. and Jesse R. "Baldy" Gruver, set up their cable tool rig on the Wheeler farm. The Gruver brothers, like Slick, hailed from Pennsylvania. They had learned the drilling business while working in Sistersville, West Virginia, and they had also taken part in the Robinson, Illinois, boom. By 1911 the two brothers had made it to southern Kansas. They were eager for work when Tom Slick offered them the job of drilling the Wheeler well. The Gruvers accepted and charged the standard rate of four dollars per foot of well. This covered the cost of their tools, labor, and living expenses. The drillers and their crew lived in tents at the well site. One night, while gathered around the campfire, Jesse Gruver commented that he did not believe they would find oil with this well. Slick, who was there checking on progress, overheard this remark and angrily denounced Gruver's pessimism. He waved his hand over the plat map and snapped at Gruver, saying that he had utmost confidence in the well and that they would find oil there.[35]

Because of the severe winter weather the drilling proceeded slowly, but by February 28 the well had reached a depth of 1,400 feet.[36] The *Cushing Independent* reported, "Wednesday at a depth of 1400 feet on the F. M. Wheeler place the drill found oil sand with what appeared to be an abundance of oil . . . Messrs. Slick and Jones contemplate casing the oil off in this well and going on down with the hole to something over 2000 feet to the second sand. This demonstration shows however, that there is oil in this vicinity."[37] The oil sand encountered was known as the Layton sand, but Slick hoped to find a more prolific sand deeper, so he kept drilling.

The well generated a great deal of curiosity and anticipation. As early as February 8 one Cushing newspaper reported that representatives of the Milliken Oil Company were observing progress and obtaining a few leases.[38] The paper cheerfully noted that "it looks now as though Cushing had the luckiest day in her history when [Tom Slick] came this way. Present prospects are that Cushing is about to enter upon an era of progress and prosperity such as has been enjoyed by many oil towns."[39]

To prevent unwanted speculation in land around the area Slick took precautions to keep his activities secret after the well had reached the Layton sand. Slick roped off the well site and posted guards to keep spectators and speculators at a distance.[40] He also kept the drilling log secret and ordered the driller to reveal the progress to no one. Slick took still another measure by building a wooden fence around the drilling site.[41] The owners of the well refused to talk about the situation. This raised suspicions even higher. As one reporter for the *Bristow Record* commented, "everybody connected with the Hi-Grade oil company has been as silent as a clam."[42] But all of Slick's actions failed to produce the desired results (except in the Tulsa newspapers). Interest in the well remained intense.

On March 17, 1912, the Wheeler well came in as a gusher, although very few people knew it at first. Slick lowered the casing in order to cut off the flow. The driller also pumped mud and water into the hole to stifle the flow of oil. Then he placed an inverted wash tub over the hole and set a large drill tool weighing several hundred pounds on top of it.[43] The moment the well came in Slick rushed to Wheeler's home. As Blanche Wheeler Kersey, daughter of Frank Wheeler, recalled years later, her father was quite angry when Tom Slick banged on the door early that Sunday morning in 1912. Then when Wheeler opened the door—Slick rushed into the house and cut the telephone wire.[44]

The Wheeler well came in during the early morning hours, perhaps between 3:00 and 4:00 A.M. Slick realized that he would have to act quickly to forestall the actions of other oilmen. One tactic was to instruct his men to belittle the oil flow as being quite small, and if pinned down "to say that a 25 to 50 barrel show had been found."[45] But at least two witnesses knew better. One recalled that "black oil was coming up, maybe 55 to 75 feet. It was way above the wooden derrick. A strong wind was blowing everywhere. [Our family] had to stay far back or get sprayed."[46] The other witness saw the well after the driller had partially subdued it, saying the well erupted "every seventeen minutes for several days lifting the obstruction [the wash tub and heavy drill tool] and throwing out about two barrels at each convulsion."[47]

After several days of waiting, news and speculation regarding the strike spread. Enthusiastic oilmen and speculators flocked to Cushing to obtain leases and otherwise participate in the coming boom. But when they arrived in Cushing they discovered that Slick had taken additional steps to restrict competition and to insure that he and his partners obtained the best leases. Slick had done something that was probably never repeated in any other oil field. After clipping the telephone wire at Wheeler's home he rode to town and throughout the surrounding countryside hiring all of the livery teams and farm wagons he could find. Then he hired all of the notary publics for his exclusive use.[48] A reporter for the *Oil and Gas Journal* told how these tactics handicapped him and two other reporters from the Tulsa newspapers (the *Daily World* and the *Democrat*) in their efforts to get a story on the well. The discovery was in a heavily wooded area. It was in undeveloped country without roads. Besides, they could not rent a livery rig because Slick had tied up every conveyance. One reporter noted, "It was a walk, and trekking out and back was a real job. When we got to the well, it was fenced off and visitors told to keep off."[49]

With these safeguards in place, Slick, Jones, Shaffer (who had arrived in Cushing when the well neared completion), and J. K. Gano, Shaffer's new lease man, began leasing all available property. Since some of the farmers were only tenants, the oil men dispatched six men to obtain leases from the owners.[50] They also had the foresight to hire men in the local area to hold leases for them. When Slick and Jones gave these men the signal that oil had been discovered, they validated the leases.[51] This allowed Slick, Jones, and Shaffer to beat their competition to the choice acreage outside the immediate vicinity of the well. Meanwhile, the delaying tactics had the desired effect. Harry Sinclair's lease man was thoroughly frustrated as he reported the situation to Sinclair:

> You see, sir, Slick and Shaffer roped off their well on the Wheeler farm and posted guards and nobody can get near it . . . I got a call yesterday at the hotel in Cushing from a friend who said they had struck oil out there. A friend of his was listening in on the party line and heard the driller call Tom Slick at the farm where he's been boarding and said they'd hit. Well, I rushed down to the livery stable to get a rig to go out and do some leasing and damned if Slick hadn't already been there and hired every rig. Not only there, but every other stable in town. They all had the barns locked and the horses out to pasture. There's 25 rigs for hire in Cushing and he had them all for ten days at $4.50 a day apiece, so you know he really thinks he's got something. I went looking for a farm wagon to hire and had to walk 3 miles. Some other scouts had already gotten the wagons on the first farms I hit. Soon as I got one I beat it back to town to pick up a notary public to carry along with me to get leases—and damned if Slick hadn't hired every notary in town, too

. . . Slick had leased everything solid . . . except some Indian leases. I've been checking the records and you have to get the Interior Department to put them up for sale.[52]

The strategy had worked. A Cushing newspaper reported, "Mr. Slick and his associates hold leases on nearly 'every thing in sight' and they are not selling."[53]

Slick's actions had the additional effect of forcing the other lease-seekers to pay much higher prices. On average, Slick paid one dollar per acre, with bonuses paid to those who owned property close to the well. By mid-April when the Indian leases became available, Harry Sinclair paid $8,000 for a forty-acre lease ($200 per acre). The Prairie Oil and Gas Company paid $6,400 for a forty-acre lease ($160 per acre).[54]

Defrauding Indians of their lands or their royalty rights proved to be another disturbing feature of the scramble for leases in Creek County. Tom Slick did not have a hand in this chicanery. But an interesting story that exemplified such abuses of Indian land rights concerned Slick's partner, B. B. Jones, and a full-blooded Creek woman named Aggie Wacoche. (Slick held the lease on the allotment of Johnson Wacoche, Aggie's husband.) Two companies and two oilmen all eagerly sought her lease. On April 29, 1912, Aggie Wacoche would "reach her majority"—that is, it would be her birthday and she would be able to sign leases for her own allotment rather than have a guardian perform this for her. One of the oilmen, Dennis J. O'Connor, sent two of his leasemen to "persuade" Aggie to sign. Seven days before her birthday they "induced" her and her husband to go for a ride with them. They took Aggie and her husband to an accomplice's home near Holdenville, Oklahoma, and later to Oklahoma City. There the leasemen bought them gifts and gave them small sums of money. They remained there until the night before Aggie's birthday; then they boarded a late train, "which would take them through Creek County at about three o'clock in the morning. . . . When the train crossed the line into Creek County in the early morning hours of April 29, 1912, [the Wacoches] were aroused, a fully prepared lease presented to and executed by them to Mr. O'Connor." They were then released and allowed to return home. Later that day B. B. Jones convinced Aggie that the lease she had signed earlier in the morning would probably be annulled and that she should sign a valid lease with him. She did so, and the commissioner of Indian affairs condemned the O'Connor lease and approved the lease with Jones.[55]

Meanwhile, the Wheeler well owners had already legally obtained the best leases, and Shaffer announced their full intention to "unveil" the "mystery well," as the press had nicknamed it. But reporters for the Tulsa newspapers, farther removed from the excitement at Cushing, were still not convinced the well would be worthwhile. The *Tulsa Daily World* noted that a portion of the well had caved in and that "interest in this well is rapidly declining." Later, the newspaper stated that the well had been cleaned out "and really ought to give a good account of itself after all the excitement it has caused . . . The majority seem to think that the well will flow from the start, although it may not amount to much in the long run."[56]

As if to convince the skeptics, Shaffer made the well log public on April 1, 1912. It provided an account of the drilling which most oilmen could appreciate:

> Water well dug to 125 feet
> Sand for hole full of water 230–256 feet
> Water sands 315 to 340, 375–380, 400–422, 450–475, 495–570
> Sandy Lime 665 to 675
> Sand 700 to 725
> Sand and water 1030 to 1065
> Lime 1417 to 1423
> Layton Sand 1423 to 1507
> Lime 1742 to 1745
> Gas Sand 1850 to 1875
> Cleveland Sand 1895 to 1960
> Top of Wheeler 2194
> Oil sand 2197
> Break in Sand 2201
> Sand yielding oil 2204 to 2208.[57]

The successful completion of the Wheeler well set in motion the Cushing-Drumright oil boom, which opened one of the largest fields ever discovered in the United States. Slick played a major role in the development of the field, which had an impact on the state economy and national petroleum market. His success marked a turning point in his life. For some reason Slick's luck changed. Behind him were the dismal failures that had earned him the unflattering nicknames "Dry Hole Slick" and "Mad Tom Slick." After Cushing, he began an incredible eighteen-year span of good fortune. Of course he continued to drill dry holes, but mostly he hit pay sand. For this he won the appellation by which most oilmen remembered him—"King of the Wildcatters." Slick's life of hard work and determination was beginning to pay dividends by leading him from "rags to riches." His admirers from Tryon noted his success with the Wheeler well: "Our old friend Tom Slick the oilman has struck it rich . . . Slick has been plugging away for several years and has put down several dry holes . . . He deserves this success and here's hoping that it will make Tom his millions."[58]

"Well, I'll Be D———d!"
TOM SLICK IN THE CUSHING FIELD

*Mike began to get restless, I could see the signs
every day. Money was rolling in; we had enough
proven acreage to drill about two hundred more
wells; but he wanted to sell out and move. He never
did get any kick out of drilling in proven territory;
he always wanted to drill wildcats and find new
oil. . . . Money has always been a by-product with
Mike—the thrill of discovery has been his chief
goal.*

Joe Trees (on Mike Benedum)

*While others scrambled for the few remaining leases in the immediate area
of the Wheeler strike, Slick, Jones, Shaffer, and Wrightsman solidified their
holdings, established their offices, began new wells, and continued drilling
those in progress.* For about ten days after the well came in, the four men
secured leases on most of the acreage within a six-mile radius. By the time
competitors could get transportation to the field and notaries to formalize
their transactions, most of the choice land was taken. But only one well,
about which little was known, had been completed. Many oilmen waited to

see which newspaper's prediction would prove correct; from Tulsa came word that the well "may not amount to much in the long run," while a Cushing paper proclaimed, "It is just a sure thing that is all."[1]

Slick and Shaffer established their office in Cushing a few days after finishing the Wheeler well. They rented the John Hopkins building for a supply storeroom and leased office space on the second floor of the Oder building, above the Cushing Drug Company.[2] This helped convince local citizens that the oil boom would be what they called "a sure thing." But the beginning of two new wells did even more to boost such optimism. Within one week after the Wheeler strike drilling began a mile south, in what would become the town of Drumright. Drillers located the other site on the Maloney farm, approximately one mile southeast of Cushing.[3]

However, the completion of the other test well (begun at the same time as the Wheeler well) truly magnified the importance of the oil find near Cushing. Reporters noted that Slick and Jones awaited the arrival of Wrightsman so that he could witness the event. On March 28, with all the owners present, drillers completed what they expected to be a gusher but what turned out to be a tremendous gas well rated at five million cubic feet per day. This helped convince a few more skeptics about the oil prospects for the area, with one Cushing paper warning that local businessmen must prepare themselves for the anticipated rapid growth but that they must not frighten potential investors by charging exorbitant prices.[4]

Meanwhile, production at the Wheeler well stabilized at a rate of about 100 barrels per day. To handle this and expected production from other wells Slick and Shaffer began constructing storage tanks near the well site, one small tank for 250 barrels and two tanks with a capacity of 1,600 barrels each.[5] This, plus earthen storage pits, held the oil until Prairie Oil and Gas completed its pipeline to the area.[6] Yet Shaffer must have handled many of these arrangements, for in early April Tom Slick suffered a family tragedy that deeply affected his life for the next year.

Upon receiving word that his father had been hospitalized in Pittsburgh, he and his brother Jesse (who had been working for Tom) left for Pennsylvania on April 11, 1912. Five days later Johnson Slick died of stomach cancer.[7] This loss upset Tom and exacerbated the physical stress he had experienced during his last four months of work. After he returned to Cushing he plunged into a frenzy of activity.

When he returned in early May the partners began four new wells, all within one mile of the Wheeler well, and continued work on those in progress.[8] Results of some of the earlier tests became known by June and helped confirm the magnitude of the emerging pool. Two more gas wells came in, one rated at ten and the other at thirty million cubic feet per day. The big news, however, was the completion of the well on the Ollie London farm for 330 barrels of oil per day, confirming the existence of a genuine pool in the area.[9]

Success quickened the pace of activity. The *Oil and Gas Journal* reported a bewildering array of combinations among the partners in drilling for June and July of 1912: "Hi-Grade Oil Co.'s No. 1 on the [Lizzie] Mikey farm; the Slick & Shaffer test on the Wacoche farm; Slick & Shaffer's No. 1 Sulloly Jones; Slick & Shaffer's No. 1 Magnolia Mikey; Slick & Jones have a rig up on the Robinson Mikey farm; Slick and Shaffer have a rig up on the F.B. Krapp farm; Hi-Grade Oil Co. had made a location on the Polly Derrisaw farm; Slick & Jones have a rig up for No. 1 Sam Dix; Slick & Shaffer have made another location for No. 2 on the [Wheeler] farm; Slick & Jones are anxious to drill a well on the Hannah Powell farm."[10]

This tangle of drilling combinations began to unravel as the partners seemed uncertain regarding their exact percentage of interest in each well, who procured the numerous leases, and the circumstances under which they were obtained. Shaffer clearly had the most at stake and consequently filed a lawsuit against Slick and Jones. He filed the suit in equity at the United States District Court at Muskogee on August 2, 1912.

All leases in the name "Slick," "Jones and Slick," or "Shaffer, Jones, and Slick" proved to be the source of conflict. Shaffer contended that Slick was his employee and, therefore, all leases taken by him rightfully belonged to the employer. He produced a contract, dated March 8, 1911, which hired Slick to procure leases in Oklahoma at a salary of one hundred dollars per month. Shaffer agreed to pay for all expenses and Slick agreed to "give his entire time and attention to the business" of obtaining leases for Shaffer.[11] Thus, Shaffer demanded that Slick assign all leases and all of his interests in leases (excluding the one-eighth to which the contract entitled Slick to keep) over to him. This land, of course, involved some of the best acreage in the emerging pool. Shaffer further complained that Slick used business expense money for his personal use and profit.

Naturally, Slick denied the charges. He maintained that regardless of what the contract required, he had always been free to take leases in his name when he paid for them with his own money. He and Shaffer had a verbal contract to this effect, and this had been in force for years prior to their agreement of March 8, 1911. Slick only viewed the written contract as a document that formalized the verbal one. He pointed to the fact that in the last several years he had drilled numerous wells with various partners and without complaints from Shaffer. For example, the Mannford well of 1911 had been drilled by Slick with Shaffer and several others serving as partners.

Therefore, Shaffer knew that Slick took leases in his own name and even backed him in drilling ventures on this land. Shaffer also had made the loan to drill the Wheeler well on the condition that Slick assign to him an interest in some of his leases, once again proving that Shaffer knew of Slick's individual leases. The most obvious sign of all that Shaffer understood the legality of what Slick had done was that Shaffer filed the suit as a matter of equity rather than one of law.[12] Any additional leases that the court might award him could prove valuable; thus the risk in court might be worthwhile. Slick viewed Shaffer's action as simple greed.

While other oilmen speculated about the outcome, negotiations between the lawyers for the three men began almost at once. The *Oil and Gas Journal* made its point of view known when it reported that "without knowing anything of the merits of the case and going into any discussion of [the] matter, [we know] that the Cushing field owes its existence to the optimism of Mr. Slick, who spent thousands of dollars near the present development trying to bring in a field and he has consistently preached Cushing to every one who would listen."[13]

By September 17, 1912, the lawyers reached an agreement to settle the dispute out of court. Some of the key provisions in the settlement included: 1) All leases would be awarded to the person in whose name the lease was taken, except for those in the name of "Shaffer, Jones, and Slick." The agreement evenly divided these lands between Shaffer and Jones since they had paid for them. Those leases in the name of "Slick" or "Slick and Jones" remained in their possession. 2) Slick would receive one-eighth of all acreage in Oklahoma that Shaffer held instead of having a one-eighth interest in these leases. This would reduce tensions and obviate any disputes over shared leases. 3) Shaffer had to pay all costs involved in maintaining leases obtained for him by Slick (such as bonuses, fees, annual payments, and so forth). Slick and Jones had to do the same for leases held in their names. 4) The agreement stipulated that any "3-way deal" between Slick, Shaffer, and Jones was invalid and the contracts should be destroyed. Each one had to disclaim all rights or interests to any lease that the others held (not including Slick and Jones for leases that they held jointly). 5) Slick gained full ownership of all Canadian leases that he had taken in Shaffer's name. 6) Slick and Shaffer agreed to cancel fully their debts to one another.[14] The two thus completely severed their business relationship, and their friendship as well. As one writer of the day observed, "The settlement leaves Mr. Slick in very comfortable circumstances so far as acreage is concerned, and the opinion is general that the settlement was good for both sides."[15]

Although now in "comfortable circumstances," the events of the previous months had exacted a heavy toll from Tom Slick. The death of his father, the intense activity of developing the Cushing field, and the pressure of the Shaffer lawsuit all combined to bring him to the verge of a physical and nervous breakdown. His own letters revealed his sorrow over the loss of his father when he wrote "perhaps some time the shadows will lift." Or the following week when he stated, "I hadn't better go home at this time as I would be sad the first time home and I can't stand any of that at this time."[16] Tom Slick, Jr., later described how hard his father had worked during these months. His father must have impressed on him just how difficult the job had been. During one interview Slick, Jr., commented on his father's strenuous work four times: "it was a very difficult job," it had been "a great effort," "it took really a tremendous strain to get those leases together," and again, "he had worked so hard up to that time."[17] Slick's physician, Dr. Emery W. King from Bristow, warned him that he could not continue at such a pace and recommended an extensive vacation.[18]

Before Slick could take such a long vacation he had to put his business affairs in order. His holdings and production had expanded steadily as the Cushing field grew through the summer of 1912. For some unexplained reason he did not want to place his brother in full charge of his business. Jesse was the oldest of the Slick children. He had worked in the oil fields of Kansas and Oklahoma and began working for his brother sometime shortly after the Wheeler strike. And while Tom trusted Jesse to manage some of the drilling aspects, he turned most of these duties over to his regular drilling superintendent, Mood Hughes.[19] Nor did he trust his brother to manage the financial affairs of the business. Instead, Tom took what must have been an unusual step for the time and placed his sister, Flored Slick, in complete charge of his oil business finances. Flored, or Flo, had graduated from Clarion Normal School in 1905 and taught at a local school until 1912. Slick probably asked her to handle his affairs because of her education and because he trusted her more than he did Jesse.[20]

This situation occurred just as the Hi-Grade Oil Company was being dismantled. The owners—Wrightsman, Slick, Jones, and his brother E. L. Jones—basically had operated independently of each other, yet they had shared interests in many of their leases. Therefore, they decided to sell their various leases and go their separate ways. They reached this agreement before Slick's extended vacation but did not set the price or consummate the deal until after his departure.[21]

Fortunately, two letters of Slick's personal correspondence documented this significant episode of placing his sister in charge and the events leading to his absence while the Cushing field entered its boom period. These letters, written to his mother and sister, reflected his physical stress, his sadness over the loss of his father, and the pressure surrounding his separation with Shaffer. He clearly realized that he was on the verge of a nervous breakdown. The letters contained a curious mixture of instructions to his sister for managing affairs and emotional statements about his condition and his life. Another letter, written by Jesse, confirmed Tom's condition and his need for rest.

In the first letter, dated September 18, 1912, the day after settlement of Shaffer's lawsuit, Tom asked his mother and sister not to worry about his safety as he planned to visit the Orient. He wrote, "I was very much disappointed when I could not get you on the phone. I can hardly go without seeing you. Don't worry for there is not as much danger as in crossing a street in the city. It will be a grand trip, and I think it will help me as my mind is sick, and it affects my body." He continued, "If anything should happen always remember that I have tried to live up to what I thought was right before God, for mans idea of right or wrong I care nothing. I care nothing for this [life] at this time, but perhaps some time the shadows will lift." Yet even in this outpouring of emotion Tom Slick, ever the oilman and lease trader, could not resist some final orders: "If Duff can't sell his share of oil on these leases he takes over, you sell it and give him half of what you get. . . . I hope Duff takes a few more of these leases as it will save me [from] spending so much. Of course I will probably make less too. He must take them as soon as he goes out or else the deal is off."[22]

The second letter, written only nine days later, contained most of the final instructions to his sister and was probably the last letter he wrote before leaving. He told his mother and sister that "Jess is down here today and I am getting ready to make a trip. I must go and the doctor thinks I hadn't better go home at this time as I would be sad the first time home and I can't stand any of that at this time. He says for me to go away and not write any letters or receive any and to forget that I have any trouble. Now I will have to leave things to you folks." He continued with instructions to Flo, "I enclose a Power of Attorney for record at Sapulpa Okla. send one dollar with it. The recorders name is H. H. Adams." Giving specific financial directions, Tom wrote, "Now it may be if the first well I drill [since his separation from Shaffer] don't come in good we will have to sell a piece or [two]. Don't get the price too low but sell when you need to. Any time you can sell the whole thing for $300,000 . . . profit let it go. I owe the First State Bank of Bristow, Okla $2000 which is due Nov. 7. Pay this and if I don't borrow money to operate with, you will probably have to sell a piece or two, Jess can find the best buyer." He further instructed her, "Don't give no options or sell on time, get the cash. Don't sign any papers that you don't know what they are, if you need an attorney get Irwin Donovan at Muskogee and have him go over it with both you and Jess. If I had enough money to drill a couple of wells I could run along all right as the oil would pay. Sign all notes that Jess sends you or gives you in favor of the Supply houses. Borrow what money you need from the Banks in Clarion [Pennsylvania] if you can or else some where else. If you can't get what you want, sell something for the most money possible."[23]

Much of the remainder of the letter dealt with arrangements made to induce his sister and mother to come to Oklahoma and with his own explanation as to why he had to take the long trip. "I must go and I may have to take a long rest. I hope you and Mother want to come out. You will enjoy the winter, you can go back when it gets hot. You would help to keep Jess doing right. And you may know I worry about leaving Jess in full charge of this property. You know how he has done in the past." He offered Flo "$75 a month if you [his mother] and her come out here, and I will pay your expenses out. If you want to stay at home I will give Flo $50.00 a month and all she will need to do will be see that the check she signs covers Okd bills or the pay roll. If this don't suit [you] I will give more for she is the only one I can depend on. I want her to take it. Jess will be glad to have you. . . . I am going to raise Jesses salary to $150 more than he is worth and tell him there is to be no board charged so Flo will be ahead the $75 . . . and I will give her more later." Near the end of the letter he continued the instructions, writing, "I allow Jess to draw on my acct. when he attaches freight or express bills to the draft of check. I sent the power of Attorney direct for record, have Flo sign the enclosed card T. B. Slick by Flored M. Slick so they can know her signature."[24]

Tom tried to reassure his mother, in the closing lines of his letter, that he would get well and that he needed to leave.

> Now don't worry if you don't hear from me, for I will be all right, if I weren't I would let you know. It is my nerves and heart. And I must give all my time to getting well. . . . Don't know where I will go but won't stay in one place after I get tired of it. I will pay you just what you want, I am working more for you folks than I am myself for I could sell tomorrow for all I ever need. I need very little for I have no interest in any thing that takes money. I think [Flo] will like the work. Now don't worry if you don't hear from me. If any thing happened to me you would hear at once as I always carry papers. I am going to get well no matter how long it takes or how much I lose. It always makes me sad when I think of things while writing and it hurts me.[25]

Two days after Tom penned this lengthy letter to his mother and sister, his brother Jesse wrote to them and confirmed many of the arrangements. Jesse explained, "Now Tom has wrote Flo, in regards to coming to Cushing [offering] her $75.00 per month but if it is a question of money, he will pay her $100.00 or even more, I will be very busy and Flo can be a great help for me. . . . Mamma here is the Idea, Tom is a [physical] wreck and he is going away until he is well he said if it took two years." Jesse also tried to convince them to come to Oklahoma, writing, "Now he has turned this all over to Flo and I to look after and I need her, and you come with her. Tom said to tell you, you both could go east for the summer. Now folks Tom has lost his health for what he has and we must keep his business for him and me looking after business, and Flo the money and we will get along all ok. You see it takes too much time," Jesse pointed out, "for all these things to get to Pittsburgh for Flo to sign and back here. Now folks we must all help each other . . . to do [justice] to Tom. Now I am getting a 5 room house with a bath and will have plenty of room, now Mamma Tom and I have made all arrangements so you and Flo will have no expense out here, all has been fixed up for that."[26]

With all details settled, Tom Slick departed for what became a trip around the world. He sailed east from New York in late September and by December had arrived in Africa. From Port Said, Egypt, he wrote a note to his physician, Dr. King, who reported that Slick was having a "splendid trip."[27] From there he went to the Orient where he traveled for a few more months, spending some of the time in China. Finally, in May 1913, Slick arrived in San Francisco and began his train ride back to Oklahoma.[28]

The most significant event to occur in his absence, besides the growth of the Cushing field, was the sale of all Hi-Grade Oil Company leases to Prairie Oil and Gas. The company's leases sold for one million dollars on March 10, 1913. The leases produced a daily average of 2,500 barrels of oil, but the sale included both developed and undeveloped areas. Of the sale price Wrightsman received half, B. B. Jones and his brother shared a fourth, and Slick got the remaining fourth.[29] These properties, however, represented only a portion of Slick's total holdings in the Cushing field.

Tom Slick really had no idea how much his holdings had been developed during his eight-month absence. Upon his return during the last week of May 1913, his brother took him for a ride through the oil field. A newspaper reporter who accompanied them gave an account of what transpired: "'Well I'll be d——d!' These four emphatic words with the exclamation point exhausted the vocabulary of T. B. Slick . . . when he beheld the Cushing oil field for the first time this week. Slick seemed dazed. He pulled off his hat, ran his fingers through his hair, and then stood with his hat in his hands behind him,

Tom Slick in China, 1912–13. Courtesy Western History Collections, University of Oklahoma Library

looking at the wide stretch of oil derricks—most of them black with oil—and listening to the chugging of gas engines and the hiss of steam . . . 'This is yours and that's yours and there's yours,' said his brother."[30]

Indeed, the list of well completions during Slick's absence revealed the extent of his success. The *Tulsa Daily World* recorded the bare facts for his prolific wells. From the Fulsom lease, and several others, Slick produced an average of more than 1,000 barrels per day. However, the most productive wells were on his Derrisaw leases, which flowed in excess of 3,400 barrels daily.[31]

The success that Slick, Shaffer, Jones, and many others enjoyed proved to be a bonanza for Creek County and the surrounding area, especially for Cushing and the budding town of Drumright. Even though the center of the action was twelve miles to the east, Cushing came to dominate because it had the facilities and the services necessary to obtain oil field supplies, such as railroads, banks, and drayage companies. Not surprisingly, prices on consumer goods rose to exorbitant levels and real estate prices jumped 30 percent and higher.[32] Other signs of significant growth at Cushing included the increasing number of automobile and livery services, a post office deluged with mail it could not deliver because of understaffing, three newspapers, a population growth from 1,500 to 5,000, and the construction of oil refineries.[33] Cushing's dream of prosperity seemed fulfilled.

The emerging boomtown of Drumright, named for Aaron Drumright, on whose land the village grew, experienced rapid growth from marginal farming and grazing land to a town of two thousand with people "living in tents and shacks scattered among the blackjacks."[34] One newspaper correspondent made numerous colorful notes on the activities and changes in Drumright. He described the town as a tiny community nestled on a timbered hillside overlooking Tiger Creek. From the emerging town one could see "the tree-clad wintry ridges and a sky-line saw-toothed with oil derricks." In another account he noted that "everything suddenly starts from nothing . . . [Then] tents go up, bunks are built, blankets are spread. . . . Rigs are set up, the engine fired, and the big steel drills go pounding their way to the depths below. Oil is struck, and news of it runs like wildfire to the other oil fields. Other operators come trooping in."[35] The reporter went on to recount how the discovery of oil enriched the farmers who leased their land and then earned royalties on the oil. He told of the poor roads, a billiard table that served as a makeshift post office, and shabby living conditions. The first homes in Drumright were little more than shacks. Lumberyards at Cushing could not get materials quickly enough to meet the demand. He estimated that at least three hundred tents were occupied as dwellings.[36]

Shelia Hawkins, the newlywed wife of an oil field worker at Drumright, described living conditions and the housing shortage there. She told of her arrival and her first night at a rooming house, which was "another name for the dump," where she shared a bed with another couple. After a few miserable days her husband made a wonderful discovery: he "learned about a tent for sale already furnished, consisting of a real iron bed, homemade table, . . . a small stove which served for cooking also heating. . . . It had double wool blankets tacked around the walls to keep cold out."[37] Some oilmen provided accommodations for their workers. After an area proved itself to be productive they might build shelter for them. Tom Slick had a row of "shotgun houses" constructed for workers, which became known as Wheeler Camp. Shaffer provided a similar facility known as Deep Rock Camp.[38] However, building such camps was uncommon, and Slick did not repeat this in any other oil boom episode. Most oil field workers had to provide shelter for themselves.

In the year after the opening of the Cushing field, an inspector for the United States Bureau of Mines, Raymond Blatchley, toured the area and witnessed with disgust another feature of the early oil booms—the waste of oil and gas. Even though his figures were most likely exaggerated, Blatchley reported the horrifying waste of natural gas, noting "the waste from the whole field may aggregate 1,500,000,000 cubic feet," as of November 1912.[39] Operators used some of the gas to fuel their drilling equipment and piped some gas to towns for home and industrial use after completion of pipelines. Most, however, simply allowed the gas to dissipate, or they might flare it to prevent its accumulation in low-lying areas.[40] Another observer described how these natural gas torches burned continuously and illuminated the entire district.[41]

Blatchley noted an equally appalling waste of oil. "A cotton field was covered with oil for one-fourth of a mile in all directions. When the wells are completed, the gas blows the oil high into the air, whence it is carried by winds over the adjoining land."[42] A newspaper reporter provided a graphic, almost romantic, description of the waste the gushers caused. He wrote that "oil runs in the ditches; escaping gas shimmers in the sunshine, and on the hills are brown patches where the oil has gushed over the top of the derrick and come down in a golden torrent [where it escapes] at the rate of 76 cents a barrel until the well has been choked into submission."[43] In addition to ditches, much Cushing oil spilled into creeks and rivers until the flow of oil from wells could be diverted into earthen storage pits or other tanks. Even stored oil constituted a form of waste since tanks and pits were uncovered, thus allowing rapid evaporation. Once the lighter components evaporated, a thick, useless sludge remained. A less conspicuous example of waste included the improper plugging of abandoned wells. This allowed underground levels of salt water, oil, and fresh water to mingle.

Slick became involved in one of the first disputes over this wasted oil. The controversy arose when W. E. Nicodemus and George Maddox constructed a dam and a trap to catch oil floating on Tiger Creek just south of Slick's Robinson Mikey lease. They diverted this oil into an earthen reservoir and by April 1914 they had impounded about six thousand barrels of oil, worth about five thousand dollars.[44] Slick sought an injunction against the two men to restrain them from pumping the oil from Tiger Creek, claiming he had the sole right to produce and sell oil from the lease. Nicodemus and Maddox countered that they held an agricultural lease that entitled them to all surface rights on the land where they had constructed the reservoir.[45] The court apparently ruled against Slick, as these skimming plants continued operation and more were built. One Drumright resident stated that "he had seen oil . . . run down . . . Tiger Creek two and three foot deep." Skimming plants north and south of town would trap the oil, then sell it to refineries. In times of shortage he claimed the people operating these traps "would pay some pumper maybe ten dollars, twenty dollars to go out there and turn a tank of oil loose, [letting] it go down the creek so they could pick it up."[46] As the Cushing field expanded northward, some enterprising entrepreneurs, among them Congressman Bird S. McGuire of Tulsa, constructed three traps on the Cimarron River.[47]

Another form of waste that most producers, including Slick, practiced was overdrilling. Fewer wells could have produced the same quantity of oil, with less escaped gas and spilled oil. On one lease at Cushing, Slick completed a well good for six hundred barrels daily. On the adjacent lease Shaffer drilled the offset well, which came in dry. Angry with these results, Shaffer moved the rig to the property line, or two hundred feet closer to Slick's producer. Not to be outdone, Slick erected a new rig near the line also. The wells were so close that when Shaffer's drillers dumped the slush from their well, the natural drainage carried it onto Slick's land. Slick notified them that this would not be tolerated, and a court order stopped Shaffer's progress. Meanwhile, Slick finished his well as a producer and thus forced Shaffer to abandon his, since state rules forbade drilling so close to a producing well.[48]

A paradox of the time was that amid the waste emerged one of the early attempts at conservation in the Mid-Continent field. The effort came in the form of a "shut-down agreement" among the cooperating producers. By this arrangement the participants (including Sinclair, McMan Oil, Slick, B. B. Jones, Gypsy Oil, Prairie Oil, and others) would shut down all drilling wells once they reached the top of the producing oil sand. Work would then be halted for about four months.[49] Not everyone adhered to the agreement for the full length of time, and the experiment was short-lived. Admittedly, the primary purpose of this agreement was to raise the price of oil by curbing production, but moderate conservation resulted as a beneficial by-product. However, sincere conservation measures required full cooperation by producers, a change in attitude toward government regulation, and an enforcement agency with clearly defined powers.[50]

In addition to developing production in the Cushing field, Tom Slick engaged in several other related ventures. The first involved the drilling of a water well for the town of Chandler in Lincoln County, about twenty miles south of Cushing. In October 1911 Chandler's city council issued a notice that it would begin accepting bids to drill an artesian water well.[51] At this date Slick had not found much oil but believed he could at least find water. Besides, the ten-thousand-dollar payment for drilling the water well would provide him with enough cash to drill more oil wells.

The first indication that Slick was interested in the water well project came on March 8, 1912, only nine days before the Wheeler well strike, when

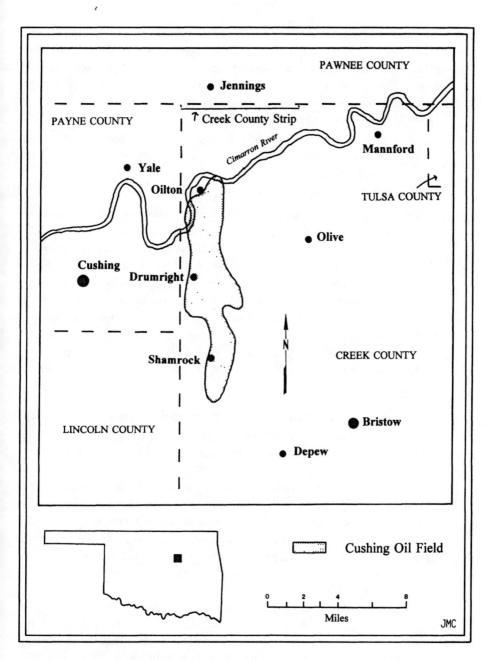

The maximum extent of the Cushing field

a Chandler newspaper reported that he had visited the area to begin assembling a block of leases. Apparently Slick agreed to drill the well, plus four others, if the city council would help him assemble a 15,000-acre block of leases. The paper encouraged this with articles informing the citizens that they could only win if they leased their land to Slick. He would find water or oil; either of these would benefit the town.[52]

When news of the Wheeler well spread, people grew excited over the oil possibilities for Chandler, and the council began securing leases. Slick became elated as well at the prospect of having such a large block of leases. He had this notice printed in a local paper:

> Oil news! Five wells for Chandler and vicinity. Don't lease your land until you see my undersigned representative. There are a few speculating scalpers after leases but we can not expect them to drill a well. Don't lease to the scalpers. I guarantee five wells for Chandler and vicinity; one to be drilled at Chandler City; one northeast; one northwest; one southwest; and one southeast of Chandler, providing the farmers in these respective localities will bunch their land into four blocks. Phone to your neighbor and tell him to look out for the scalpers and not lease to them, as I am the one who will put down the wells at once. Have developed Cushing field and will do the same for you. Must have the assistance of every loyal citizen. Leases must be in the name of T. B. Slick, A. B. Oleson [the mayor], or A. A. Mascho [a city councilman].[53]

Slick even visited Chandler on April 9, 1912, to discuss his scheme with the city leaders. His plan and the reasoning behind it was similar to that at Tryon eight years before. He demanded the large block of leases "to keep others from profiting from a field developed by him."[54]

After numerous delays Slick and the city of Chandler finally entered into a contract to drill "a deep well, ostensibly seeking artesian water but in reality a prospect for oil or gas."[55] Under the terms of the agreement, Slick, after posting an $8,000 bond, would select a site within the city limits to drill. Once the well reached a depth of 2,500 feet he would receive $9,000 in payment and a bonus of $1,000 if he drilled the test to 3,000 feet. He had to begin drilling within ninety days.[56]

Slick easily met the deadline, with drilling commencing on July 10, 1912. He attended the "spudding in," confident that the well would find gas, oil, or water. Slick, the affable promoter, told those present that the well might be drilled as deep as 3,500 feet and that they would find "China or oil."[57] This optimism slowly vanished over the next nine months as the drillers experienced numerous problems with the well. In February 1913 they reached the depth of 2,500 feet but continued drilling the test. Two months later the well collapsed, crushing the casing and forcing abandonment of the well.[58] Therefore, Slick received the $9,000 payment but he did not experience firsthand the disappointment of the Chandler townspeople, for by this date he had not yet returned from his trip around the world.

Another of Tom Slick's business ventures during the Cushing boom involved the massive waste of gas that so appalled inspector Blatchley. In July 1912 Slick and his friend B. B. Jones asked the Cushing city council for a franchise that would allow them to furnish the city with gas. Slick and Jones would lay and maintain the pipelines, set meters, and charge a rate of twenty-five cents per thousand feet. In addition, they would supply gas, free of charge, to city hall, ten street lamps, and all churches in town.[59] The franchise, subject to the approval of city residents, received a resounding endorsement in a vote of 162 for and only 3 against.

However, the state supreme court had ruled earlier that public utility franchises could not be granted to individuals, only to corporations. Slick and Jones immediately incorporated themselves as the Cushing Gas Company. They also purchased the materials and a warehouse near their newly established office.[60] Yet before their project advanced very far the partners decided to sell their business. Two Pittsburgh entrepreneurs bought the franchise for an undisclosed sum and changed the name to the Creek County Gas Company.[61]

Another short-lived venture by Slick and Jones concerned the construction of a refinery at Bristow. This plan emerged in July 1913 when Slick had about 4,500 barrels of daily production and Jones had a similar amount. Both men were disgruntled because refiners could make five times as much profit on a barrel of oil as producers. With this in mind, Slick made a trip to New York City to arrange financing for their proposed 5,000-barrel capacity refinery. Several weeks later the two men gave up on this plan (for unknown reasons), much to the dismay of Bristow citizens.[62]

These various business efforts remained peripheral to Slick's central interest in discovering and producing oil.[63] But even his desire to do this seemed somewhat diminished after his return from worldwide travel. As he surveyed his vast holdings Slick felt that the excitement of discovering oil—that thrill of winning a contest against nature—had vanished. Within several weeks of his return he began secret negotiations with Roxana Petroleum Corporation to sell all of his Cushing holdings.

According to the news reports of the day, "representatives of a large oil company" met Slick as he stepped off the ship in San Francisco and offered to buy his oil properties. This most probably was Roxana, for as early as May 20, 1913, (the week he returned) they had inspected his holdings at

Cushing.[64] Slick did not wish to sell his property at this point, but by August, just over two months after his return from traveling, he offered to sell all his acreage to Roxana for $5,000,000. Roxana officials thought this price was too high and countered the offer with a much lower one of only $1,500,000. Slick then offered his producing leases only for the reduced price of $3,000,000. The oil company sent the superintendent of its American division, N. G. G. Luykx, to Tulsa to negotiate directly with Slick. Luykx succeeded in obtaining an option on all of Slick's holdings for $4,000,000, but the option expired before Roxana officials took action.[65]

One month later Luykx returned to Tulsa to assess the value of Slick's holdings and to make another offer. But on September 1, 1913, Slick made a three-point proposal: to sell his 1,725 acres of proven leases for $2,000,000; to sell selected tracts of this same land for $1,800,000; or to sell virtually all of his acreage, proven and unproven, for $2,500,000.[66] The last point seemed the best offer, and Roxana promptly dispatched two more representatives to gauge Slick's production. They determined this to be about 3,000 barrels daily.[67] However, with the Slick deal pending, Roxana purchased an oil company in California and because of this could not afford the Cushing property. Nevertheless, Roxana made a final offer of $1,750,000. Slick refused.[68] The company's skepticism over the value of Slick's property seemed justified when estimates of his daily production declined to about 1,500 barrels in December.[69]

To help him in his search for a buyer, Slick employed the services of Percy D. McConnell, a well-known broker of oil properties. McConnell quickly arranged a sale to the Carter Oil Company for the price of $1,500,00.[70] Slick agreed to sell because he too feared the value of his property might be declining. But the deal raised a question concerning Indian leases. Before Indian lands could be leased to oil prospectors, the Bureau of Indian Affairs (BIA) had to approve each lease. The bureau further regulated the amount of Indian leases held, ruling that "no person, firm or corporation will be allowed to lease, within the territory occupied by the Five Civilized Tribes, for the purpose of producing oil or gas, more than 4,800 acres of land in the aggregate."[71]

Generally, Tom Slick avoided taking leases on Indian lands. At the beginning of the Cushing boom he had avoided them because he wanted to maintain secrecy and because he had to act quickly. Bureau "red tape" meant that neither of these purposes could have been accomplished had he gone through BIA procedures. During his entire period of interest in Creek County, from 1910 to 1920, Slick owned no more than fifty Indian leases, and it appeared that many of the leases that he did take were on assignment. This meant that someone else took the lease, gained BIA approval, then sold, or "assigned," the lease to Slick.[72]

Nevertheless, from 1911 to 1913 Slick had acquired several Creek Indian leases. Eighteen of these, totaling more than 2,400 acres, were involved in the proposed Carter sale. Indian Superintendent Dana H. Kelsey expressed concern that "of the 20,000 shares of stock of the Carter Oil Company, all but 50 shares are owned by the Standard Oil Company of New Jersey." He reported moreover that the same persons who controlled Standard also owned 93 percent of the stock of Prairie Oil and Gas Company. Kelsey then proceeded to explain the connection between the three companies: since Carter "is practically owned by the Standard . . . they, of course, will produce oil for their own refineries, and as the Carter Company has no pipe lines, nor available method of . . . transporting it to the Standard refineries, except through the Prairie Oil and Gas Company, that whatever oil they produce will be sold to the Prairie Company."[73] The Prairie, with its large Indian lease holdings, had already reached the 4,800-acre maximum. Thus, by treating both companies as Standard subsidiaries, Standard, under whatever name, could only hold 4,800 acres. On December 10, 1913, the commissioner of Indian affairs, Cato Sells, rejected Slick's sale to Carter.[74]

Unable to find an acceptable buyer at a suitable price, Slick kept his Cushing properties a while longer. Fortunately for Slick, the property he could not sell eventually earned the fortune he used to finance his moves into other fields a few years later. His Cushing acreage, though it suffered a temporary lag in production, rebounded and made him a multimillionaire. What made the Carter sale denial particularly fortuitous was the fact that it nearly coincided with the discovery of the Bartlesville sand of the Cushing field. Prairie Oil and Gas found this prolific sand, which dwarfed production from the shallower Layton and Wheeler sands, on November 30, 1913.[75]

Slick commenced to deepen some of his wells that had minimal production in the shallow sands and began to drill more wells. Newspapers recorded his progress for the first nine months of 1914 as a period of extraordinary success. Wells producing more than 1,000 barrels of oil daily became commonplace. A few of his biggest wells included Johnson Wacoche No. 1 at 1,050 barrels per day, the No. 3 at 1,400 barrels per day; Miller Tiger No. 6 at 950 barrels daily; Isaac Wacoche No. 4 at 1,000 barrels per day; Eliza Lowe No. 2 at 1,850 barrels daily, the Nos. 3 and 5 both at 1,900 barrels per day, and the No. 4 at 2,160 barrels daily. Some of Slick's most prolific wells were on the Robinson Mikey lease where the No. 6 came in at 1,008 barrels, No. 4 at 3,000 barrels, No. 11 for 5,000 barrels, and the No. 3 for 6,000 barrels of daily production.[76] As one writer noted, the mundane task of reporting daily oil production actually had an incredible aspect to it when viewed in literal terms. He gave as his example, "T. B. Slick's No. 5 Miller lease in 17-17-7 is good for 800 barrels natural. Have you ever stopped to think what that means? Can you picture an incident in the great commercial development of a country that increases a man's income $800 a day to be dismissed by the newspapers in two or three lines? Yet that is what it means to Mr. Slick. . . . He is drilling wells all over the Cushing field and is bringing in big ones, so that by next January he will rank among the richest men of the nation."[77]

With such tremendous production Slick needed a storage facility. He and B. B. Jones agreed to build a tank farm and railroad loading facility near Bristow. Slick and Jones, as well as many other producers, agreed that this type of storage would allow them to store their oil until prices rose. These higher prices for oil would easily offset the costs of building the tanks. The partners purchased two hundred acres south of Bristow and began constructing storage tanks. Slick also laid a pipeline to carry his production from the field to the tank farm. To accommodate this increased oil business, the St. Louis & San Francisco Railroad (generally called "the Frisco") built a spur route to the tank farm and loading rack.[78] By mid-August the completed facility went into operation with twelve 55,000-barrel tanks. One month later Slick alone shipped an average of twenty-five railroad tank cars of oil daily.[79]

Amid this flurry of activity Tom Slick once again felt the strain of overwork. It was likely that he had never truly recovered from his breakdown of 1912. Even in 1913, only seven months after his tour around the world he cited poor health as his reason for wanting to sell his Cushing acreage to Carter Oil Company. In a letter from U.S. Indian Superintendent Dana Kelsey to Commissioner of Indian Affairs Cato Sells concerning the proposed sale, Kelsey twice mentioned Slick's ill health as a mitigating circumstance in favor of approving the sale. Now, once again, Slick took an extended vacation to rebuild his health. He went to England in late August 1914 with a friend also engaged in the oil business.[80] When Slick returned he renewed his efforts to dispose of his holdings. In September, with Slick's cooperation, John T. Milliken of Saint Louis formed a syndicate known as Slick Oil Company. Chartered under Colorado laws on September 10, 1914, the new business offered Slick $2,500,000 for most of his Cushing holdings, and he accepted. Milliken owned half of the new company, Okla Oil Company held a fourth while four Pittsburgh men controlled the remaining fourth.[81]

Once again, however, they had to submit the deal to the Bureau of Indian Affairs for approval since Slick still had the same Indian leases. The bureau studied the proposal in detail. At issue was the one-fourth owned by Okla Oil. As bureau officials discovered, Tidewater Oil Company of New Jersey owned virtually all of Okla Oil. Standard Oil in turn owned approximately 42 percent of Tidewater. For eleven months the bureau debated whether Standard-Tidewater-Okla connections provided an unfair advantage in violation of the 4,800-acre limitation. On July 22, 1915, the bureau issued its decision stating that Standard's percentage of interest in Indian land would be negligible and, therefore, approved the sale.[82]

Other oilmen complained bitterly that the acreage limitation rule had been violated. One writer commented sarcastically, "Surely, the interior department moves in mysterious ways its wonders to perform, as is evidenced by the recent action in approving the transfer of the Oklahoma oil properties of Thomas B. Slick to the Slick Oil Company." He then complained that "a few months ago a deaf ear was turned to the plea of 20,000 persons . . . [who had signed a petition to the Secretary of Interior requesting that he] modify the departmental regulations so as to permit the acquiring in excess of 4,800 acres in restricted Indian leases, and yet right on top of that refusal comes the announcement of the approval of the Slick transfer, in which the Standard Oil Company is interested as a stockholder."[83] Most oilmen soon realized the decision might work in their favor by setting a precedent that they could use to force a modification in the acreage limitation rule. To this end a group of Osage land lessees hired the same lawyers who had engineered the Slick transfer. The most notable lawyer was a former congressman from Pennsylvania and future attorney general of the United States, A. Mitchell Palmer.[84]

Even though he sold most of his property, Slick kept some scattered acreage, "just enough to keep him busy," and temporarily retired from the oil business. The Cushing oil boom had provided one of the most exciting episodes in Oklahoma's history. It provided numerous jobs, brought millions of investment dollars, heightened awareness of the need for adequate conservation legislation, made the state the leading oil producer from 1915 to 1917, raised the standard of living for many, created dozens of millionaires, and made a legend of Tom Slick. He must be given credit for discovering the field, although many others made contributions, including Charles B. Shaffer, B. B. Jones, Charles Wrightsman, Josh Cosden, John Markham, Jr., Harry Sinclair, and companies including McMan, Prairie, Roxana, Gypsy, Magnolia, Empire, and Producers.

The Cushing field helped make the United States a major petroleum producer. For a time the tremendous volume of Cushing oil crippled the U.S. market by driving prices as low as forty cents per barrel. In terms of international importance Cushing supplied a major part of the petroleum products that, together with the Healdton field of Oklahoma and the El Dorado field of Kansas, helped the "Allies float to victory on a sea of oil." Cushing, at its peak, supplied more than 60 percent of the high-grade refinable crude produced in the Western Hemisphere—some 300,000 to 330,000 barrels per day.[85]

The Cushing boom also dramatically affected Tom Slick. Here he achieved his goal of becoming a millionaire, but it likewise helped define a pattern that he followed the remainder of his life. Though his entry into other oil fields may not have been as spectacular as Cushing, he continued to move into new areas, always as an independent, and to obtain a significant amount of the production. But once the thrill of discovery evaporated and he had worked himself to the verge of physical collapse, he would sell most of his interests and take a vacation. Then, once he recuperated, or when someone offered him an irresistible deal, he would return to the oil game with a vengeance. He never learned to balance work and leisure.

In-Law Entrepreneurs

*Lady Luck seems to take revenge on all great pros-
pectors who are unfaithful to her. Almost without
exception, whenever they attempt to take their
winnings from the gaming table to invest in something "secure," they lose.*

Ruth Sheldon Knowles

*In 1891 the Illinois Central Railroad hired a restless but experienced, young
man named Joseph A. Frates as a dispatcher for its station in Water Valley,
Mississippi.* While there he befriended a co-worker named B. B. Jones. After
a few months each received a promotion and moved. Frates eventually
went to work for the St. Louis & San Francisco Railroad (the Frisco), as
chief dispatcher at Springfield, Missouri.[1] Jones moved to Bristow, Oklahoma, to join his brother in banking and real estate. Jones also became a
backer, partner, and friend of Tom Slick. In 1915 Frates went to Bristow to
explore the possibilities of building a spur route from the Frisco station there
into the Cushing oil field. He and Jones renewed their friendship, and Jones
took the opportunity to introduce his bachelor friend Slick to Frates's eldest
daughter, Berenice.[2]

After a brief courtship, Tom and Berenice set their wedding date for October 1915. He hoped that by then the pending sale of his Cushing properties would be approved so he and his new bride could enjoy a honeymoon.

*Berenice Frates Slick, circa 1917. Courtesy Western
History Collections, University of Oklahoma Library*

The couple had to alter their plans, however, when Tom's brother Jesse suffered a serious illness. They advanced the wedding date so that they could travel to Clarion immediately and await the outcome of Jesse's illness.

The couple exchanged vows on June 21, 1915, at Berenice's home in Springfield, Missouri, with Reverend John T. Bacon of the Cumberland Presbyterian Church presiding. One society column writer noted, the bride "wore a stunning traveling gown of blue and gray cloth with kid trimmings, which was extremely becoming. The accessories were in harmony."[3] They departed at once in her father's private railroad car and went as far as Saint Louis. From there they continued to Clarion and stayed in their new home until Jesse recuperated. Afterwards, the newlyweds spent several months traveling.[4]

Tom Slick's new wife came from a well-known family in the railroad business. Joseph A. Frates began working for the Southern Pacific in 1882 at Martinez, California. There he learned to use the telegraph. Frates put his new trade to use in dozens of locales in California, Mexico, Arizona, New Mexico, Nevada, Texas, Colorado, Mississippi, Tennessee, and Missouri. While in Leadville, Colorado, in 1889, Frates met and married Lula M. Buck. The following year their first child, Berenice, was born.[5]

Frates began working for the Frisco in 1902 and eight years later became general superintendent for their lines between Saint Louis and Oklahoma City. During the next several years Frates noticed that the Frisco lost a large amount of freight tonnage into the oil fields and the lead and zinc mining areas of Oklahoma. Local drayage firms at stations along the main rail line transported these raw materials, supplies, and passengers to and from these regions. Frates suggested to the Frisco management that they should build extensions from their main trunk line into these areas to exploit the great volume of traffic. The president of the Frisco agreed, but the weak financial condition of the company would not permit such expansion.[6]

Frates believed that he could raise the money needed to build a short extension line into the burgeoning oil fields from Depew to Drumright. He received a loan and, with financial support from five other partners, began building the Sapulpa and Oil Fields Railroad in 1915.[7] The construction of this line brought Frates to Creek County, where he met his old friend Jones and his future son-in-law Tom Slick.

Slick had just gone into virtual retirement from the oil business after the sale of his Cushing properties and had just married Frates's daughter. He could also see the instant success that his new father-in-law enjoyed with the short line railroad. Few were surprised then when Slick and Frates announced plans to begin their own rail line into the rich lead and zinc mining region in Ottawa County, Oklahoma. The two men also planned to purchase plantations in central Mississippi. These plans marked a dramatic new phase in the life of Tom Slick because the nature of these businesses was so different from oil. During the next several years, Slick's various enterprises proved to be successful, in contradiction to Knowles' maxim quoted earlier, and he kept many of the businesses until 1929. But privately he must have longed for the excitement of exploring for oil. Even so, he embarked on these new ventures as the in-law entrepreneurs built railroads, established towns, and operated plantations.

On June 21, 1916, Slick and Frates made arrangements to become partners and build a railroad into the world-famous Tri-State District of Missouri, Kansas, and Oklahoma. The timing of their venture seemed auspicious since demands for lead and zinc reached high levels during World War I. Munitions manufacturers used both of these minerals as components in their products. This rapid increase in demand taxed the transportation network in the Tri-State District.[8] Frates and Slick sought to exploit this deficiency and build their own line into the area.

Frates resigned from his position with the Frisco; then he and Slick proceeded to acquire and survey land for their line. The two men reached a friendly understanding with Frisco officials whereby they leased construction materials from the Frisco. In exchange, the two men agreed to pay an annual rental fee of 6 percent on the value of these materials, to route all traffic possible to the Frisco, and to give them exclusive purchase rights should they decide to sell at a future date.[9]

Slick and Frates formed their new company in February 1917 and called it the Miami Mineral Belt Railroad, or the Mineral Belt. The board of directors consisted of only five men: J. A. Frates, Sr., president; J. A. Frates, Jr., general manager; J. H. Grant, secretary; with Slick and William Matthews as vice presidents.[10] Regardless of their titles, two things became clear—Frates, Sr., managed the company and Slick provided much of the capital. Of the 2,000 shares of stock that the new corporation issued, Tom Slick owned 1,996, while the remaining officers owned one share each.[11]

The surveying for the Mineral Belt began in March 1917, with construction following immediately. Frates's own company, the Oil Field Short Line Construction Company, built the first segment of the line.[12] Tracks for the Mineral Belt commenced from the Frisco line in Quapaw, Oklahoma. They ran generally west and north to Picher. Passing through several of the mining camps such as Century, Douthat, and Cardin, the line occupied a strategic position in the core of the Oklahoma sector of the Tri-State District.[13] By June the Mineral Belt carried its first shipment of ore from the mines to the Frisco tracks at Quapaw. The owners then planned to add passenger service as well.

Crews finished construction to Picher in June. Passenger service began on July 4, with a large celebration marking the event. Frates later wrote of this occasion: "The running of the first through passenger train from Quapaw to Picher on July 4, 1917 was a gala event. The train, composed of engine, combination baggage, mail and express car, and five day coaches, was loaded to its utmost capacity, and the citizens of Picher and nearby mining districts were apparently all on hand to aid in presenting a befitting reception."[14]

The Mineral Belt enjoyed immediate success. Newspapers noted the heavy freight traffic, especially at Picher, where "the yard tracks . . . were filled with cars loaded with freight."[15] At one point in July the Mineral Belt had three hundred cars of coal awaiting delivery. The Miami newspaper noted, "The Miami Mineral Belt . . . is handling an immense tonnage to the mining fields of Ottawa County. The Mineral Belt is handling every car turned over to it by the Frisco and M.O. & G., and maintains an excellent freight schedule." The report continued, "This line is doing a great deal to relieve the freight congestion in this district, and while it cannot handle as much business as it

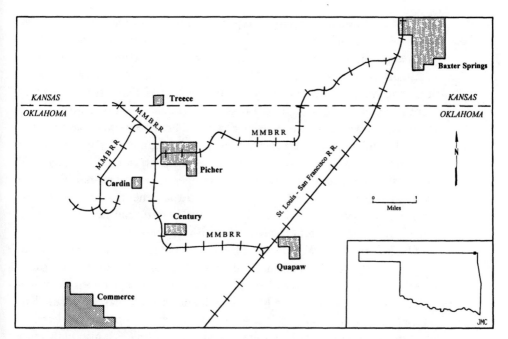

The Miami Mineral Belt Railroad

will when its branches and sidings are completed, the Mineral Belt has handled a great deal of freight the last few days."[16]

The volume of business no doubt exceeded the expectations of the owners. One Mineral Belt official commented anonymously, "We have started and can't stop. . . . We intended to stop building at several points, but the mine owners farther on would give us no rest."[17] Therefore, the Mineral Belt owners planned to expand in three directions from the line's western terminus at Picher. First the rail line would move south through Commerce to Miami. Frates and Slick never completed this portion of their line. The next extension would move northward into Treece, Kansas, and continue on to Columbus where it would connect with the Missouri, Kansas, and Texas Railroad. This segment of their extension was completed only as far as Treece. The third extension, and the only one fully constructed, moved in a northeasterly direction along the state boundary line, then crossed and entered Baxter Springs, Kansas, from the west. Here the Mineral Belt intersected the Frisco once more. Much of this extension construction was done in 1918 and early 1919.[18] Besides the major additions, the line built spurs or sidings for almost every mine in the area. In October 1917, one company official declared the Mineral Belt had "completed spurs to about fifteen mines at the present and we will have switches to about sixty within thirty days."[19]

In addition to carrying freight, the Mineral Belt provided other services. In August 1917, company officials contracted with the United States Postal Service to carry mail to the numerous mining camps along its lines, such as Douthat, Century, Cardin, and Tar River.[20] The major business other than freighting, however, was the passenger service. Frates observed that the Mineral Belt "did a thriving business from the very beginning. During the first three or four years it operated four regular passenger trains daily and handled up to 1800 passengers per day."[21] The passengers consisted primarily of mine workers who preferred living in the nearby towns rather than in camps. This service continued to prosper until two electric interurban railways entered the territory and undercut the Mineral Belt's business.[22]

Overall, the Mineral Belt proved to be a profitable venture for Slick and Frates, even though the line remained relatively small. With only about thirty miles of track, the line provided important connections between the mines and the major railroads. The Mineral Belt transported coal, mail, supplies, and workers into the mining camps and returned with ore and workers. At one time, the line employed about three hundred people.[23] It also built spurs into most of the mines, thus allowing quick and efficient removal of the mineral ores. The Mineral Belt produced great profits for the owners, paying stock dividends for one six-month period of $57,190. Most of this went to Slick since he owned virtually all of the stock. The other officers earned salaries. With their success and profits Frates and Slick turned their attention to a new railroad venture into the oil fields south of Tulsa, but the two men maintained ownership of the Mineral Belt until 1929 when they sold the line to the Frisco for $43,317.48.[24]

Their next railroad, built in Creek County, served much the same purpose as the Mineral Belt—to tap a new area unserved by the larger railroads. Slick and Frates incorporated their new line, named the Oklahoma Southwestern Railway (OSWR), in January 1920.[25] This new line served the Fox, Slick, Bristow, Phillipsville, and Youngstown oil pools of the region. Another key purpose of the line was to provide rail service to the new towns of Slick and Nuyaka in the oil boom area. The OSWR had the same basic organization as the Mineral Belt in that Frates supplied the railroad managerial knowledge while Slick provided most of the financial backing.

Construction of the OSWR began in March 1920. Crews graded the roadbed in a southeasterly direction from Bristow. Local citizens grew excited at the prospects that the OSWR might become a major railroad with planned

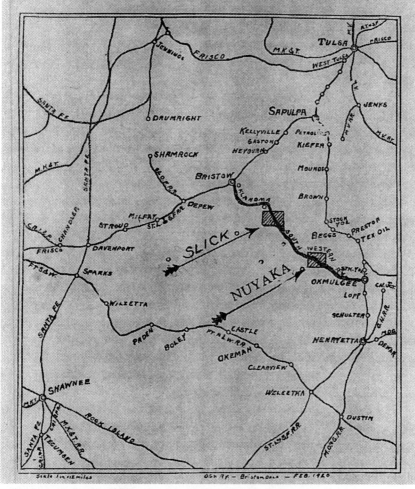

SLICK, OKLAHOMA
12 Miles from Bristow. 14 Miles from Kelly-
ville. 14 Miles from Beggs. In the heart of
the new Slick Oil Field.

NUYAKA, OKLAHOMA
12 Miles from Okmulgee. 12 Miles from Slick.
10 Miles from Beggs. In the heart of the Phil-
lipsville-Youngstown Oil Field.

Both Surrounded by Unsurpassed Agricultural Lands. The Oklahoma-Southwestern Railway, now
Operating Trains into Slick and Nuyaka, and under construction to Okmulgee, making Both Acces-
sible to the Great Marketing Cities of the State.

*The reverse side of Slick Townsite Company stationery displayed
this map of the Slick-Nuyaka area. It showed the Oklahoma
Southwestern Railway running from Bristow to its proposed eastern
terminus at Okmulgee. Courtesy Thomas B. Slick Collection,
Western History Collections, University of Oklahoma Library*

construction on into Okmulgee then to Seminole and south to a point on the Red River in Jefferson County. Such a line would have cost several million dollars; therefore, Slick and Frates abandoned this notion.[26] Instead, they built a modest railroad from Bristow to Nuyaka, a distance of about twenty-four miles. Sixteen gangs of men worked on the railroad daily to build the line as quickly as possible. The Bristow newspaper commented on the quality of the materials and machinery used to construct the railway, observing that this was "the first new railroad in Oklahoma that has ever been laid with 90-pound steel" tracks.[27] As a time- and labor-saving device, the crews of the OSWR used a new rail laying machine invented by employees of the company.[28]

By July 25, the OSWR reached the town of Slick. The railroad, along with a new highway, gave local citizens adequate transportation, which many locales in the state sorely lacked, especially the oil boom areas.[29] Within a few months the railroad extended to Nuyaka, but it was never completed to its proposed eastern terminus at Okmulgee. When completed, the OSWR provided freighting and passenger service for the bustling oil fields and farms. It carried oil field equipment, new residents, construction materials and consumer goods into the area while it transported oil and farm goods out to the main Frisco line in Bristow.[30]

For the next four years Slick and Frates gradually expanded and consolidated their railroad holdings into a small transportation empire. In 1922 Slick purchased the Oklahoma Union Railway (OUR) and Interurban Construction Company, which operated an interurban line between Tulsa and Sapulpa. The company also owned street railroad lines in both of these towns and a smaller interurban line between Sapulpa and Kiefer (six miles south of Sapulpa).[31] Next, Slick and Frates consolidated the OSWR and the OUR under the latter name and moved all of their railroad offices, including those for the Mineral Belt, to Tulsa in June 1923.

The *Tulsa Daily World* described the impact this move had on the city with its headline "Half Million Dollar Pay Roll Brought Here by Slick." The paper declared that the railroads employed 259 people with an annual pay roll aggregating $500,000, "making this city the nerve center of a group of enterprises destined to play an important part in the future growth of Tulsa."[32] The new offices occupied twenty-one rooms in the OUR terminal and additional space in the First National Bank building.

The offices expanded in 1924 when, under Frates's initiative, the two men formed the Union Transportation Company (UTC). Since interurbans were becoming less profitable, Frates and Slick organized this new company, which provided bus service. It carried passengers to points beyond the limits of the OUR and eventually supplanted all of the OUR interurbans in the Tulsa area. It also provided bus service between Tulsa and Holdenville, Oklahoma (about ninety miles south of Tulsa). At its peak of operation in the late 1920s, Frates estimated that the UTC transported about six million passengers annually.[33]

Throughout all these various transportation ventures the same basic partnership existed between Tom Slick and his father-in-law. Slick provided the bulk of the money while Frates supplied the expertise and additional capital. Frates and several subordinates managed all of these ventures. Slick did take part in the management of the railroads—for example, he engineered their purchase of the OUR—but he left most of the responsibilities to Frates. The two men maintained their railroad holdings for about thirteen years until they sold them to the Frisco in 1929 for an undisclosed sum.[34]

As stated above, one motivating factor for constructing the OSWR in 1920 was to provide transportation to another Slick and Frates enterprise—the new townsites of Slick and Nuyaka. Both men had experience at this particular type of business venture. Almost eight years earlier Slick participated in boosting a new town in western Creek County, and only four years before, Frates had established a new town in Kay County, Oklahoma.

The first news of the proposed town of Exeter appeared in the hectic days after the completion of the Wheeler well. One Tulsa newspaper reported that Wrightsman, Slick, and Jones planned to establish the townsite in the Tiger neighborhood near the well in anticipation of the coming oil boom.[35] A Cushing newspaper noted that, "It has all along been the intention of the parties who are developing this oil field to promote a town site at this place."[36] Wrightsman apparently selected the name Exeter for the new town because his son attended the academy so-named in Massachusetts.[37]

By the end of May 1912 the new site exhibited a few signs of growth. One of the only surviving descriptions of the oil town noted, "The oil camp Exeter is situated on a wooded hill mid way between the Wheeler well and the gas well. It contains about a half dozen tents and as many . . . newly constructed and neatly painted buildings. Here a ten foot piece of pipe elevated from a pipe line merrily burns escaping gas day and night."[38] The town failed to grow any larger though and a few weeks later the same newspaper announced "the town of Exeter is being moved this week, bag and baggage, to the Fulkerson farm," which was then evolving into the town of Drumright.[39]

Frates's experiment with town building enjoyed slightly more success. He organized the Dilworth Townsite Company in January 1916. Dilworth, in northern Kay County, was near an emerging oil pool. Frates built the Oil

Field Short Line Railroad from a nearby point on the Frisco to serve the new town. He also provided utilities for the community with his Dilworth Power and Light Company.[40] The town prospered only as long as oil was produced, then it faded, although it still could be found on a 1988 Oklahoma road map.

In the first weeks of 1920 Slick and Frates completed plans to build two towns in the developing oil boom areas between Bristow and Okmulgee. These plans, in conjunction with their Oklahoma Southwestern Railway, would provide communities where workers could reside, services could be based, agricultural goods could be marketed, and profits generated for the townsite company owners. In March 1920 Slick and Frates organized the Slick Townsite Company.[41]

The new company, operated in a manner similar to their railroads, had Frates in primary control with Slick providing more capital than guidance. The site selected for the new town was about twelve miles southeast of Bristow on the Little Deep Fork of the Canadian River. After surveying and platting the 240-acre tract, the owners liberally advertised that the town named in honor of the oilman by his father-in-law would open on March 15, 1920. One advertisement proclaimed that Slick would be "a mecca for wide awake, progressive business men who are ever on the lookout for better locations for their business. This new town is jammed full of excellent opportunities." The town, in a "great forest of oil derricks," had the equal fortune of being surrounded on all sides by "fine agricultural lands. . . . This town means new blood and new opportunities. Only live, up-to-the-minute residents are wanted in Oklahoma's newest town. If Horace Greeley was alive today, without a doubt, he would advise, 'Go to Slick, Young Man, Go to Slick.'"[42]

The town opened with great fanfare at 9:00 A.M., Monday, March 15, when company officials raised an American flag on a pole in the center of Main Street. The sale of property commenced immediately as business lots sold for one thousand dollars while residential lots cost two hundred dollars each. Advertisements encouraged investors to "buy to the limit of your pocket book" with terms of one-fourth down and the balance in ten equal payments. As an added incentive, no payments were required if the purchaser became ill or lost his job.[43] Frates later remembered that "several hundred lots were sold" on that day.[44] Prospective customers arrived at Slick to find red, white, and blue streamers marking the lots. Signs labeled streets named for generals such as Pershing, Foch, and Funston and with avenues named for universities, such as Princeton, Harvard, Yale, Cornell, and Columbia.[45]

The town of Slick experienced the phenomenal growth typical of boomtowns. As entrepreneurs and residents constructed shops and houses,

Booster advertisement for the town of Slick.
From the Bristow Record, *March 11, 1920*

lumberyards and hardware stores did a great business. The townsite company was responsible for some of the construction as they set up their offices and even built homes to sell. Within two weeks the company had sold enough lots to establish a town for four thousand people, leading a writer for the Bristow newspaper to exclaim, "The new town of Slick is growing like a new baby should, fast."[46]

The town had a temporary setback in June when a fire destroyed five businesses, causing damage estimated at $25,000, but it rebounded promptly in July when the OSWR arrived.[47] The new railroad provided both freighting and passenger services. Managers of the line set to work immediately on the depot after they completed the freight station. The passenger station, built with the same specifications as the Frisco depot in Claremore, Oklahoma, had a fashionable stucco design.[48]

After only eight months Slick had an impressive array of about a hundred businesses. The town newspaper, the *Slick Spectator,* listed the various industries, businesses, and professionals operating in October of 1920. These included the usual businesses: numerous cafes, grocery stores, lumberyards, oil-related concerns, a hospital, a bank, and cotton gins.[49] By early 1921 Slick grew even larger with discoveries of oil close to the town. In February the population had increased to about three thousand while the number of businesses doubled. One new business included a "$50,000 brick fire-proof hotel and cafe" built by the Hotel Department of the OSWR.[50]

Frates, Slick, and the townsite company attempted to provide utilities and services to keep pace with the startling growth of the town. The Slick Park provided space for public events. The baseball diamond and raised platform for boxing matches were the popular attractions there.[51] Employees of the OSWR, with the cooperation of the railroad management, installed their own hospital on the second floor of the post office building. The hospital served the employees of all Slick-Frates railroads, and the public as well.[52] A public school opened in January 1921. At the same time the townsite company decided to provide street lights, natural gas, and a power plant. One Tulsa newspaper declared that these amenities along "with the water system, which is nearing completion, will give the citizens all conveniences that can be had in any first-class city."[53]

Slick, however, was not as idyllic as the booster literature indicated. The town, built on a site once called Wild Horse Prairie by the Creek Indians, now served as the home for both wild men and women. Crime and vice plagued the new boom community of Slick just as it had countless other boomtowns. One report observed that Slick was "running wide open with gambling, booze, and prostitution," with a disreputable character named "Whitey" Payne in charge of the illegal activities.[54] Indeed, the first murder occurred within one month of the town's opening.[55]

Crime and vice were not so apparent in Slick in the early months of the town's existence. But as the oil boom grew, conditions deteriorated: "The old west, unfettered by law and conventionalities lives again in Slick." At sunset hundreds of oil field workers "in their blue shirts and khaki pants, their faces smudged with grime and dust" appeared. "Then little points of light [sprang] out here and there along the darkened streets and tin pan pianos beat a ragged jangle. . . . The pool halls, gambling houses and all of the underworld life of Slick" came to life.[56] A taxi cab driver confirmed this scenario when he wrote of his days in Slick, saying the town was "a ring tail doozy. Hammers & saws quit at sundown and 45 thumb busters [carpenters] started popping. Everything locked up, then the night dives opened up."[57]

Crime in the town reached a climax in December of 1920. During Christmas celebrations a group of inebriated men began shooting guns in the business district and soon had the meager police force intimidated. This touched off a wave of violence that lasted for about thirty-six hours. One witness described the action: "Slick, to a casual observer might have been a motion picture studio, Sunday night and Monday [December 26 and 27], with a thrilling western story being filmed. But the animation was too real to be enjoyed by spectators. Early Monday morning a bunch of men shot the windows out of a dozen or more business places and kept up a fusillade of bullets for an hour, and all day Monday there was more or less shooting and fighting in the business section of town. Hi-jackers contributed their share to the outlawry."[58] The spree ended with several people suffering gunshot wounds and with the patrons in two restaurants being robbed.[59] After these outrageous events the citizens complained to the county commissioner who sent additional officers to subdue the criminal elements and restore order.

The other town that Slick and Frates founded opened on August 19, 1920. Nuyaka, midway between Slick and Okmulgee and near the confluence of the Little Deep Fork and Deep Fork of the Canadian River, took its name from the Creek Indian mission located nearby.[60] The Nuyaka Townsite Company operated as a subsidiary of the Slick Townsite Company and had the same officers. Nuyaka was surveyed, platted, and sold in a manner similar to Slick, although the newer town was much smaller. Also, Nuyaka was billed as more of an agricultural center than Slick. However, oil and the OSWR proved to be the central focus of the town. Many of the oil-related businesses of Slick purchased lots in Nuyaka as well. But its boom was of short duration and intensity and the town never really grew.[61]

The decline in oil production led directly to the demise of both Slick and Nuyaka, although both remained viable communities for several years. A serious fire in August 1922 nearly destroyed the business district of Slick. By 1930 the population there had dropped from its peak of five thousand to less than five hundred. The OSWR was also abandoned in 1930. The decline of Nuyaka was even more precipitous.[62] Fifty-eight years later Slick still appeared on an official state road map, but Nuyaka did not.

A story pertaining to the demise of Slick involved the town's namesake and the local bank. When town entrepreneurs established a bank, they asked Tom Slick to lend his prestige to the new enterprise by becoming a stockholder and director. He agreed to do so. Several years later the bank failed and all depositors lost their money. Slick called immediately for a list of the

Tom Slick with two of his children, Betty (left) *and Tom.*
Courtesy Western History Collections, University of Oklahoma Library

depositors and the amount each one lost. As Slick explained the situation years later, "That was once I had to pay for my vanity. I didn't know anything about banking, but I'm proud of that town named after me, and when they wanted my name as a director of a new bank I was flattered and let them have it. When it failed I guessed that a lot of men put money in there simply because my name was backing it, so I paid them all, to the last penny. I did not have to, but Tom Slick couldn't afford to have that stain on his name."[63]

Another business venture by Slick and Frates involved the purchase and management of plantations in Mississippi. B. B. Jones entered into this enterprise with Slick and Frates and was probably responsible for convincing them to make this investment.[64] They made their purchases about the same time they began planning railroads in Oklahoma. In 1915–1916 Slick and Frates bought Valley, Clarion, and Oakdale plantations in Yazoo County, Mississippi. These properties covered a total of six thousand acres, each farm equipped with a cotton gin, a saw mill, barns, warehouses, farming machinery and implements, and housing for employees and tenants. They employed a general manager for each plantation. Most of the work in their first few years of ownership centered on making general improvements in the land, buildings, and personnel. One significant change was the addition of a general store.[65] Valley Plantation, the largest of the three, occupied 2,240 acres. Frates's son Clifford managed this property, which grew corn, cotton, oats, and pecans, and had 1,000 acres in pasture with 185 head of cattle.[66]

Slick and Frates no doubt played a limited role in overseeing these plantations. This venture, although it represented a substantial investment, provided few financial returns for them. Years later Frates offered this assessment: "These plantations represent an investment of about $750,000. We have never received any dividend on this investment; however, these farms are well equipped and highly improved in every particular. Furthermore, they have furnished steady employment to an average of more that 80 employees."[67]

Thus, generally from 1915 to 1920, Tom Slick became involved in several enterprises with his father-in-law, J. A. Frates, Sr. In every instance Slick remained in the background, providing the investment capital but little of the guidance. Instead, Frates furnished the leadership in managing the railroads, townsite companies, and, most likely, the plantations. Slick never revealed why he chose this secondary role for himself. Perhaps he lacked sufficient management skills, or these ventures did not really hold his interest. He may have dabbled in this wide variety of activities in an effort to find something interesting but less stressful than the oil business. Another possible reason was that this offered a way to maintain his income while he used most of his time to relax and rebuild his health. Perhaps he chose this role because it gave him time to spend with his wife while they built their family. In this general time span all three of their children were born—Thomas Bernard (named for B. B. Jones), Betty, and Earl Frates.

None of these businesses, however, held his interest the way oil had. During these years Slick drilled an occasional well and acquired scattered acreage, mostly in Creek County. One of his wells near Shamrock, Oklahoma (midway between Bristow and Cushing) brought excitement to the town's citizens, and, probably, to Tom Slick as well. While there checking on a well, Slick met another prominent oilman, Harry Sinclair. The two men enjoyed a few drinks, then decided to race buckboards down Tipperary Road, in the center of which Slick had an oil rig.[68] Basically though, Slick sat on the sidelines while the oil industry progressed during these years. But, by late 1919 he was ready to reenter the game and in a big way. Within five years he would earn his nickname "King of the Wildcatters," discovering oil pools in Texas, Oklahoma, and Kansas.

5

"To See the Oil Gush Once More"

It takes luck to find oil. . . . Luck enough will win
but not skill alone. Best of all are luck and skill in
proper proportion, but don't ask what the pro-
portion should be. In case of doubt, weigh mine
with luck.

Everette L. DeGolyer

Slick reentered the oil business in the last few months of 1919 and early
1920. Over the next five years he had an incredible streak of good fortune in
which he discovered or helped discover four pools of oil and played a large
role in developing two others. At this stage of his career he expanded his
fields of operation to include Kansas and Texas, as well as Oklahoma. Slick's
expansion coincided with a general fear that market demands for oil would
outpace the discovery of new reserves. The demand for oil increased throughout most of the 1920s as the automobile gained in popularity and as industrial and commercial uses expanded. But America's energy future remained
uncertain unless producers could find more petroleum. This basic concern,
plus the anticipation of higher prices, sent wildcatters and oil companies on
a frantic search for oil.

Tom Slick selected a peculiar location to renew his activity in oil. One year before the Wheeler well, he, along with B. B. Jones, Claude L. Freeland, and another partner, had drilled a well near Mannford, Oklahoma, on a tract of land owned by Slick and Jones. The land stretched along the northern border of Creek County like so much geographical flotsam. This peculiar tract, made up of pieces of unallotted Creek Indian lands, was about seven miles long and only three hundred feet at its widest point.[1] After failing to find oil at the eastern end of the land strip eight years before, Slick and Jones prepared to drill farther west near the newly emerging pool southeast of Jennings, Oklahoma (or about five miles northeast of Oilton).

In July 1919 the two men selected locations for three test wells. These were south of the proven productive area of the Jennings pool in an area consistently reported as unfavorable by geologists. A previous dry hole drilled nearby seemed to confirm these reports. But in November, when the first Slick and Jones well came in producing forty barrels per hour, oilmen were greatly encouraged. A Tulsa newspaper responded to the new oil find with the headline, "Thomas Slick Has His Usual Luck."[2]

A few weeks later the second well came in at an impressive rate of about four thousand barrels per day. Slick and Jones promptly began drilling more wells on the strip, eventually giving them a total of eight. All of these wells produced oil but their production decreased dramatically as other companies moved onto adjoining leases and completed offset wells.[3] The production from these eight wells faded into insignificance when compared to the wells Slick would drill during the next few years. Their true importance was that they whetted Slick's desire to return to the oil business on a full-time basis.

An Oilton taxi cab driver described an experience he had in 1920 that conveyed how Tom Slick operated and the extent to which he had reentered the oil business during these months around the Jennings boom. As the driver, Jack Weber, told the story:

In 1920 I had my taxi lined up last in line, waiting for the little bob tail passenger (AT & SF) connecting Jennings, Okla. with Cushing. This was at Oilton. A man dressed in blue overalls and jacket came along the platform carrying an over night bag, and as he came to each Driver they would turn their back to him, me being last he says, "Well, will you haul me?" "O.K." I says, "get in and where to?" "The Royal hotel." . . . He asked me to wait while he went into the hotel and I said, "Just leave your bag with me." We left there going from one lease to another all day, me getting hotter under the collar as the day passed. We wound up in Drumright that evening and my party said, "We will put up in the hotel tonight. I will pay expenses [or] if it would suit you better, I will pay you off and get another cab in the morning." "O.K.," I said, "I'll shoot the works, I'm with you." We went from lease to lease all next day stopping in Cushing that night, and the 3d night we came to Stillwater, Okla. My fare says, "now I will pay up," so I figured up 3 days driving at $3.00 per hour driving time. He payed off in double saw bucks and gave me an extra for a tip. He said, "my name is Slick, T. B. Slick."[4]

This story described a man intimately involved in the daily affairs of his business. As long as the leases were in a fairly small area, he could inspect his properties on a three-day cab drive. But as his business expanded this became more difficult, especially as he moved into Kansas and Texas.

Within a few weeks after completing the last well on the Creek County strip Slick began operations in the southeast corner of Cowley County, Kansas, about seven miles southwest of Cedar Vale and near the Oklahoma border. Slick leased the 7,000-acre Olsen ranch in December 1920, beginning drilling shortly thereafter. In taking this lease, he accomplished something every oilman hoped for: his lease entirely covered what proved to be a pool of oil. The Olsen ranch lay on what geologists termed a "well-defined structure," meaning it would very likely contain oil and/or gas.[5]

Drilling commenced on the Olsen No. 1 in January 1921 and progressed at an average pace until March when the derrick caught fire, completely destroying the rig. The possible cause of this fire became clear in April when the well came in as a four-million-cubic-feet gas well.[6] Since no pipelines existed, much of this gas was wasted, except for the trivial amount used to fuel the other rigs nearby. In fact the waste grew worse because as the drillers periodically deepened the well in an attempt to find oil, the gas volume increased. By September 1921 the Olsen No. 1 produced twelve million cubic feet of gas daily. Slick eventually sold the gas to a company, which then began piping it to the town of Cedar Vale.[7]

Since Slick controlled all the acreage, he developed the Olsen pool, as it came to be called, at a leisurely pace. His second well hit oil in February 1922. A local paper conveyed the excitement: "This is not a dream, dear reader, it is a reality. Oil, honest-to-goodness oil, is spraying over the top of the derrick from T. B. Slick's No. 2 on the Olsen ranch."[8] Their hopes for an oil boom were disappointed, however, as Slick drilled only six additional wells in the pool over the next three years. Seven of his wells proved to be of long-term value by producing oil as late as 1927.[9] Even so, the Olsen pool was clearly of minor importance. Shortly after completing the first two wells here, Slick moved much farther south to try his luck in Texas.

Eastland County, Texas, (about fifty miles east of Abilene) had been the site of the notorious oil booms at Ranger and Desdemona. In the extreme southwestern corner of the county near the tiny village of Pioneer came the next boom in 1922. Here Slick and others set in motion a flurry of activity that lasted for more than four years as the boom expanded into the adjacent counties of Callahan, Brown, and Coleman. Oilmen discovered several pools of oil in the area, but none were as spectacular, or short-lived, as the find at Pioneer.

Slick's interest in the Pioneer area began in early 1922 when Oklahoma City oilman Edward R. Wilson approached him with a deal. Wilson had heard of a well near Cross Plains (about five miles west of Pioneer) that had produced oil and gas for a year even though the hole was obstructed. After surveying the well and the area, Wilson became convinced more oil could be found nearby. He mortgaged all of his personal property and, in partnership with Pennant Oil Company of Tulsa, began buying leases. Wilson then sold much of his interest to Slick, who agreed to drill the first well.[10]

The oilmen disclosed few of the facts concerning their deal, which involved only one hundred acres of land. The tract covered portions of two farms—fifty acres each from W. J. Bryson and from B. F. Eakin. Slick controlled all of Eakin's portion and held one-half interest in Bryson's land. Undoubtedly, Slick provided much of the drilling capital, although Pennant Oil furnished its own rig for the first Bryson well. Slick constructed four rigs of his own in March 1922 on the Eakin tract.[11] For the next two months drilling proceeded at a normal pace.

A hint of the success to follow came in April when Pennant completed a good well two miles west of Pioneer on a lease unrelated to the Slick deal. Many began to speculate on the possible importance of this well. One month later its significance became certain when the Pioneer newspaper announced with its bold headlines "World's Biggest Shallow Oil Field, 7500 Barrel Gusher, Slick & Pennant Bryson No. 1 Blew in Roaring Out Bowels of Earth from 2457 ft. Sat. Night."[12] The Bryson No. 1 came in after midnight, spewing high gravity oil around the well site. Workers rushed about with flashlights as they hastily constructed storage tanks and made pipeline connections. By daybreak spectators from the local towns of Cross Plains, Rising Star, and Pioneer arrived to see the well that would bring the anticipated oil boom to their area. Citizens planned a "Big Celebration and Jubilee," scheduled on May 30 at the city park in Pioneer, to express their gratitude.[13] By that date they had even more cause for rejoicing because the Bryson No. 1 had proved to be only the prelude.

One week after completion of the Bryson well Slick's Eakin No. 4 gushed in with a spectacular amount of oil. The Eakin well, only eight hundred feet east of the Bryson producer, came in at ten thousand barrels per day. This massive production overtaxed the pipeline and required immediate action to save as much oil as possible. One eyewitness gave a vivid account of the preparations made in the days after completion of the Eakin well. "Two hundred men swung into action: teamsters, roughnecks, tank-builders and pipeliners. Holes were gouged in the ground, and dams were thrown up to create earthen storage. Steel tanks were erected and lines installed to them. Crews of sweating, cursing men rushed the construction of a large pipeline. Workers wore slickers to protect themselves from the rain of crude; and the pipeliners, in hip boots, waded in oil that was sometimes knee-deep."[14] The writer went on to say that the crews worked as much as eighteen hours a day to complete the tanks, pipeline, and earthen storage. After several days of furious activity, fifteen acres had been transformed into a "temporary lake of petroleum."

The storage problem became more acute when the well's production rose to its peak of fifteen thousand barrels daily. At this point the Texas Railroad Commission, the regulatory agency for that state, issued orders forcing Slick to curb production until pipelines could be built that would handle his large volume of oil. Prairie Oil and Gas already had three four-inch lines in place, but these failed to handle the local production.[15] Prairie officials ordered construction of an additional six-inch line, primarily to handle Slick's production from the Eakin lease. In the meantime more wells neared completion as drillers halted progress at the top of the sand and awaited pipeline connections.

In June 1922 Prairie completed the new line, and the Railroad Commission lifted production restrictions. Throughout June and July Slick continued to bring in large producers, although none were as prolific as the Eakin No. 4.[16] Ironically, the production at Pioneer began to diminish just as the commission relaxed its sanctions. For part of May and all of June Slick had an average daily production of 7,344 barrels. In the third quarter this figure dropped to 2,314 barrels and in the final quarter of 1922 fell to 1,252 barrels.[17] Despite this dramatic decline the figures remained impressive. Coming from only a few wells, the exceptionally high-gravity oil brought a price as high as $2.88 per barrel while the average for 1922 was about $1.65 a barrel.[18]

The boom was intense while it lasted. Pioneer experienced phenomenal growth during the summer of 1922, as did nearby towns. The activity attracted hundreds of workers and various entrepreneurs. The neighboring town of Cross Plains, for example, became the location for several oil field supply houses and other oil-related enterprises. Banks, hotels, and restau-

Slick's Eakin No. 4, near Pioneer, Texas, in 1922, shortly after the erection of earthen dams to hold the large amount of oil that flowed from the well. The "lake of petroleum" can be seen in the foreground. Courtesy Western History Collections, University of Oklahoma Library

rants sprang up to meet the demand. Both towns competed for the oil business that emerged near Pioneer and spread west toward Cross Plains (then south toward Cross Cut). Hundreds of wagon loads of materials were shipped into the fields from both Cross Plains and Pioneer.[19]

Grateful businessmen in Cross Plains held a banquet to honor Slick in "appreciation of the big oil wells, . . . and more especially for the interest which Mr. Slick is taking in the . . . general welfare of the City of Cross Plains where he and his associates are permanently located with their offices through which all business for this field is transacted."[20] In addition to his offices, Slick took part in another local enterprise when he and a former partner, Claude L. Freeland, completed a small refinery about one mile east of Cross Plains in September 1922. The Freeland Process Refining Company had a capacity of five hundred barrels daily and produced refined oil, kerosene, and gasoline. All of the crude for the refinery came from Slick's Eakin lease.[21]

With the oil boom progressing between Pioneer and Cross Plains, Slick's attention turned to other areas, particularly in the nearby town of Cross Cut in Brown County. Here, over the next four years, Slick helped exploit a large discovery known as the Cross Cut pool. The production from individual wells was not as spectacular as at Pioneer, but growth of the newer pool continued steadily. Slick played an important role in developing this area as he owned an interest in the discovery well that opened the pool in September of 1922. Thereafter he joined with other local oilmen to drill wells in the area. In that same month Canyon Oil (Crabb-McNeel-Bryant) and Tom Slick began drilling several wells in northwestern Brown County. Many of these wells came in as producers, thus assuring the importance of the Cross Cut pool.[22] Slick was content to let others drill these wells for him because by late 1922 his interest had shifted almost entirely to an eighty-acre lease near Tonkawa, Oklahoma, where a well he owned neared completion.

Slick bought into his next deal at about the same time as he began to drill in the Pioneer field. In early 1922 Henry Rosenthal of Springrose Drilling Company offered one-half interest to Slick if he would finance the drilling of a well on an eighty-acre lease that Rosenthal owned. Rosenthal, also from western Pennsylvania, with drilling experience in Illinois, Kansas, and Oklahoma, owned the lease on a portion of Laura Endicott's farm, near the border of Kay and Noble Counties and less than five miles south of the town of Tonkawa.[23] Rosenthal, however, found himself in a difficult financial situation and could not afford to pay for the drilling, thus his offer of one-half ownership to Slick if he would pay for the well. Slick hired at least three geologists to survey the area before he committed himself to Rosenthal. The geologists all made adverse reports on the lease, but Slick had a "hunch" and decided to play it. He agreed to Rosenthal's deal.[24]

Slick and Rosenthal's Laura Endicott No. 1 commenced drilling in February 1922. After about one month the well hit a six-million-cubic-feet flow of gas at a shallow depth. Shortly thereafter, in a spring storm, the gas ignited when lightning struck the derrick. A fire ensued and completely burned Rosenthal's rig. With mounting debts and the loss of his rig, Rosenthal agreed to sell his one-half interest when Ernest Marland asked him to do so. However, he split his interest, selling part of it to Marland and part to Slick. This gave Slick a controlling three-fourths ownership of the lease. Each new owner paid $25,000 for his new portion. One Tonkawa newspaper wrote that Slick's purchase was "believed by local geologists to be one of the best buys of the year. They declare that the one-fourth interest bought by Mr. Slick, which gave him control, is easily worth $100,000."[25]

Slick prepared to build a new rig and to continue drilling at once. Meanwhile wells began to come in on surrounding leases, further enhancing the value of the Endicott acreage. Just how fortunate his purchase had been became clear in December when the Laura Endicott No. 1 blew in at the rate of 190 barrels per hour (or 4,560 barrels per day). This success, coupled with previous big production from Comar Oil, Marland, Lew Wentz, and Gypsy Oil, touched off the great Tonkawa oil boom.

During all of 1923 Slick drilled numerous wells on the Endicott lease. Several became tremendous producers. As of March, three wells were particularly large, one for 4,800, one at 5,000, and another at 10,000 barrels per day. This large initial production came at a time when Tonkawa high gravity crude sold for the high price of $2.40 per barrel.[26] Slick and other oilmen continued to find good production in the area throughout the year at depths of 2,000 to 2,500 feet.

With such productive wells many operators never considered drilling deeper. So perhaps the most important news item of the year appeared in late June when the Tonkawa paper casually noted that Slick planned to deepen one of his Endicott wells in search of the Wilcox sand. "This is the first definite notice by any local operator or producer that drilling will be done at this depth."[27] Most believed 1923 would be a difficult year to surpass since the Tonkawa field produced more than thirty million barrels of oil and many considered the field to be on the decline. Oilmen may have thought it foolish of Slick to drill deeper. The Endicott lease, easily the most profitable eighty-acre tract of the entire field, produced 2,348,950 barrels from thirty wells for 1923.[28]

Slick's deep test attracted plenty of attention, especially as it neared depths that had produced oil in other fields. Hopes dimmed when the well reached 3,800 feet without finding oil, but papers reported that "he will keep on drilling until he gets into salt water or oil, even if it is necessary to go down to 5,000 feet."[29] On April 8, 1924, Slick's well found a high gravity oil sand at 4,062 feet. This unexpected sand immediately quieted all doubts about the efficacy of drilling the deep test. At the top of the sand, the well gushed forty barrels per hour, then slowly increased and stabilized at forty-five barrels. By week's end, after drilling another two feet, the well produced seventy barrels per hour.[30]

As news of the massive production from the deep sand spread, geologists debated its exact location and name. In the meantime, state oilmen provided a solution which proved to be permanent—they named the new pay horizon the Slick sand. Numerous telephone calls and telegraph messages to the oil editor for the *Tulsa Daily World* supported this idea.[31] Slick now had a town, an oil pool, and an oil sand named in his honor.

Naturally, this new find spurred intense drilling activity by the other operators in the Tonkawa field. Various companies selected a total of thirty-two new locations, requiring 452 wagon loads of construction materials. The increased activity stimulated business in nearby Tonkawa and other surrounding towns. The Tonkawa newspaper quipped that the Slick sand was "producing in more ways than one," with the establishment of several new businesses and "others who are looking for a location to 'Spud In.'"[32]

Though the town boomed, Slick hoped the drilling campaign would be more controlled. He suggested that Tonkawa operators drill only one well per forty acres to the deep sand, "thus efficiently and properly draining the deeper pay sand." Other goals attained by such a limitation would have included lower overall drilling costs and maintenance of higher oil prices since production would remain fairly steady.[33] This plan was far too conservative, however, and the oilmen finally agreed to a limit of three wells per forty acres. Even this limitation was conservative for that time, as the previous number in such an agreement had been four.[34]

Despite this limitation, the wells from the Slick sand produced tremendous quantities of oil, thus forcing oil prices downward. By September 1924 the price for high gravity crude had plummeted from $2.40 to $1.35 per barrel.[35] To avoid selling at the lower price Slick and other oilmen began to build storage tanks. They decided to store the oil until prices rose once again. Slick built a total of fifteen 55,000-barrel tanks near the Endicott lease. His average daily production was more than 16,000 barrels so it took less than two months to fill all of his storage tanks.[36] This tactic, plus decreased production, had the desired effect, and by 1925 prices began to climb higher.

Slick's production from the Endicott lease had indeed been phenomenal. As of January 1926 the eighty-acre lease produced 5,733,745 barrels of oil. The whole Tonkawa field had yielded more than 76,000,000 barrels, much of this from the Slick sand. The field easily earned its nickname "the Billion Dollar Spot."[37] Henry Rosenthal long regretted the sale of his interest in the Endicott lease to Slick, but such was the nature of the oil business. George Bruce, a Wichita, Kansas, oilman and friend of Rosenthal, told of business trips the two men made over the years as they traveled between Kansas and Oklahoma City. Bruce said he teased Rosenthal about turning "green" each time they passed the Tonkawa exit on Highway 77.[38]

Slick matched his success at Tonkawa with his drilling efforts in an area along the western end of the boundary separating Hughes and Okfuskee counties in Oklahoma, centering on the town of Wetumka, known as the Papoose pool. He began drilling several wells northeast of the existing field in February 1924.[39] In late July his first well came in as a monstrous gas well. This generated a great deal of excitement among oilmen, as they hoped it might prove to be an extension of the existing pool. This hope stemmed from the fact that the well was producing about 150 barrels of oil along with the gas.[40] After three months Sinclair Pipe Line Company completed a line to the Slick well to handle the production expected from this new extension to the Papoose pool.[41]

And a big pipeline was needed. During the next two months the northeastern sector of the Papoose pool gushed with oil from wells drilled by Slick and other operators such as Kingwood Oil, Papoose Oil, Prairie Oil and Gas, Independent Oil, and Cosden Oil. These companies were amply rewarded for the high prices they had paid for leases, the highest being $100,000 for an eighty-acre tract.[42] Slick bought one-half interest in some extremely valuable acreage (400 acres) from John Bott of Okmulgee. Bott later refused $2,500,000 for his half interest in the leases.[43] With all of this acreage Slick proceeded to drill a large number of wells, becoming one of the most active operators in the area. He owned 34 of the 110 wells drilled in Papoose, his being among the largest producers, with wells like the Hully Sand No. 1, 1,300 barrels; Bott-Slick No. 1, 3,168 barrels; Bruner No. 1, 3,120 barrels; and many more. As of January 1925 he had eight producing wells with an aggregate production of 12,450 barrels daily.[44]

Slick's prodigious activity in the area prompted the construction of a boomtown to accommodate the work force. The oil field workers chose to name the town Slick City. The town of Slick City was short-lived in name only, because of the confusion created in mail service. As a local newspaper described the problem, "Since the opening of the new oil town of Slick City, the mail and parcel post service and freight and express service [at Slick, Oklahoma] is in a muddle, because officially there is no Slick City, there being no post office or railway there. . . . It is not believed that Slick City will ever have a post office under that name." A few weeks later the confusion ended when the citizens agreed to change the town's name to Papoose.[45]

In the same month that Slick found the deep Tonkawa sand and moved into the Papoose pool he began his second move back into Kansas. This time his discovery of a pool there proved a bit more significant than the Olsen pool had been. His new activity, also in Cowley County, proceeded on a 1,086-acre block of land covering farms owned by three different men, W. G. Carson owning the largest portion. Slick bought this deal from a Tulsa geologist named Fred Merritt. Based on his survey of the area, Merritt believed that the acreage would produce oil and convinced Slick to drill a test well. The land was located near the center of the western boundary of Cowley County, or about two miles southeast of Oxford and seven miles due west of Winfield.[46]

Work began on the Carson No. 1 on July 3, 1924. The location held promise based on Merritt's report but also because it was only a few miles north of the Graham and Rainbow Bend pools. In light of his recent successes, other oilmen watched Slick's progress with keen interest. They thought perhaps his luck would expire with this well because in recent years three dry holes had been drilled within about two miles of the Carson well.[47] But in late September the well struck a shallow oil formation. Slick was convinced, however, that a deeper and better sand would be found, so the drilling continued.[48] Near the end of October his persistence paid off when the well hit the Wilcox sand, discovering what became known as the Slick-Carson pool.[49]

The well came in as a 2,400-barrel-per-day gusher. At the time it rated as the best well ever drilled in that area of Kansas. A large crowd gathered to witness the gusher as the drilling crew turned the great flow of oil into the hastily improvised storage pond. Slick at once ordered the construction of proper storage tanks, which would hold the oil until completion of a pipeline.[50] The newspaper for Oxford, the nearest town to the well, excitedly announced the new well: "That the end of the Rainbow so far as Oxford is concerned lies to the southeast . . . on the W. G. Carson land showering all its rich tints on a pot of black oil gold is no longer a dream of a community but an actual fact."[51]

Many of the familiar events following the completion of a discovery well occurred with the opening of the Slick-Carson pool. Slick and operators on adjoining leases began drilling new wells at once. The oilmen also scrambled for acreage at premium prices. For one nearby tract of 300 acres Slick paid $150,000. Ernest Marland spent $30,000 for 135 acres.[52] The town of Oxford benefited from the brisk activities, especially the cafes, lumberyards, and bank. Geologist Fred Merritt even moved his office from Tulsa to continue his explorations in the area. Local citizens were so grateful for Merritt's service in convincing Slick to drill on the Carson farm that they bought Merritt a new Ford coupe.[53]

The new pool meant immediate wealth for the Carson family as they received royalties on all oil produced from wells on their land. Some royalty brokers estimated that the value of the Carson farm had risen to about $1,000,000. The Carsons remained fairly unexcited at their new wealth; Mr. Carson warned, "Don't let the goldarned thing run wild and ruin a lot of wheat." One of his children boasted, "If this well turns out all right we're going to get a new aluminum tea kettle."[54]

For the next two years Slick and the other operators of the pool, mainly Carter Oil, developed the area at a moderate pace. Many of the wells came in as only average producers with about two hundred barrels daily initial production. By 1927 the pool had twenty-five wells, each with an average daily output of fifty barrels.[55]

Slick's success in Kansas capped a five-year string of good fortune from Jennings, Oklahoma, to the Olsen pool in Kansas, then to the Pioneer and Cross Cut pools of Texas, then north to the shallow and deep pay sands at Tonkawa, on to the Papoose field, and then north again to the Slick-Carson pool near Oxford, Kansas. Thus by geographically spreading the risks of drilling, Slick had managed to minimize the proverbial danger of "putting all of his eggs in one basket." By avoiding overinvestment in one area, he maximized his chances for success. He then used his production in one area largely to finance his efforts in another.

What made his widespread success even more remarkable was that he managed much of this activity simultaneously and personally. This of course contributed to his achievements and to his declining health. When asked about his success in the oil business, Slick cited his personal supervision as a key factor: "From long experience in the field I know how to drill a well to best advantage, and when I'm drilling one, and they get down to a critical depth, I am there, Johnny on the spot, and see that it's done right. Land owners know that; they know if they lease to me I'll superintend the drilling personally, and that they'll get the best service; that if there's oil I'll find it." His interviewer then queried how this could be managed when he had so many wells in progress in three different states. Slick responded, "I do it. I'm in my car, going from one well to another, watching everything."[56] Contemporaries marveled at Slick's intensity, a quality that had helped make him the most active and successful independent oilman in the nation.[57]

Slick had assistance in managing his oil empire, but he kept his staff at a minimum. When asked in 1924 if he would expand his office and staff to accommodate his vastly increased volume of business, Slick retorted, "What's the use of a flock of department heads when you've got three aces on the job."[58] Slick's "three aces" were Charles F. Urschel, E. E. Kirkpatrick, and James Huffman. Urschel and Slick had been friends for years, since their early days as employees of Charles B. Shaffer. In September 1916 Urschel came to Oklahoma and began working for Slick as the manager of his financial and business affairs.[59] Urschel also married Slick's sister, Flored. He remained Slick's most trusted friend and adviser. Ernest E. Kirkpatrick of Brownwood, Texas, met and became a close friend of Slick in 1922 when Slick first became interested in the Pioneer and Cross Cut areas in Texas. Slick invited him to "come up to Oklahoma with me and I'll make you some money."[60] Kirkpatrick had many talents: he was a "geologist, landman, lease expert and practical attorney, combined."[61] He also became a published poet. Slick hired Kirkpatrick to work as his lease man and scout. James Huffman, who Slick also met at Pioneer, became Slick's superintendent of production and field operations. This meant that Huffman supervised the drilling process and informed Slick of the progress. He made sure that all needed equipment was available and that the oil was properly stored or transported to market.[62] Other men later served Slick in that capacity, but Urschel and Kirkpatrick held their positions until Slick's death.

In addition to Urschel, Kirkpatrick, and Huffman, Slick had several other employees, designated as subsuperintendents, who had responsibility for immediate supervision of wells and production for specific areas, such as Kansas-Tonkawa, Texas, and Papoose. These employees reported to Huffman, who in turn answered to Slick. Through daily communications with his three executives Slick maintained personal control over his business operations.[63]

Besides Slick's competent personnel and his own dedication and complete involvement, he attributed his success to his thorough knowledge of the oil regions of Oklahoma, Kansas, and northern Texas. As he explained it: "I know all this oil country, every foot of it. As a leaser I drove and walked over all of it, studied it, have learned to sort of sense, by intuition, where there ought to be oil." He admitted, "I don't know it, of course; I put down many a dry hole, sink many thousand dollars, but I have been at it so long, have studied the lay of the land and the underlying formations so persistently, have drilled so many wells, dry and wet, that I often get a hunch, sort of feel that there's oil in a certain spot, and when I get that hunch I play it, lease her up and put down a hole, and if I strike oil everyone calls it Tom Slick's luck, but do you call that luck? I call it largely judgment based upon experience."[64]

Slick further discounted pure luck, claiming that oilmen must be able to recognize good opportunities when encountered. In colorful, homespun language he explained the role of luck in his own efforts: "Some folks don't recognize Good Luck when they meet it in the middle of the road. So I have been fortunate, or lucky, whichever you call it, but I've also done a lot of calling Good Luck to bring it my way. Did you ever shoot ducks? Lay hidden in a blind and call to the ducks as they fly over, and bring them within range? Same way with Luck. A whole flock of lucky chances may fly past unless you know how to call them to you, and have a good gun, all loaded, and are able to shoot straight, see?"[65]

But as Slick indicated, people tended to focus upon his tremendous and highly visible successes and ignored or did not know of his numerous failures. While he discovered pools of oil and found deeper pay sands, he also drilled dozens of dry holes all over his three principal states of operation.

Only the oil journals and the oil pages of larger newspapers silently chronicled these failures in their fine-print listings of drilling reports.[66]

Slick knew well the hazards of wildcatting for oil and had plenty of dry holes as proof. One well that he drilled in Major County, Oklahoma, offered an example of the hardships, great expense, and frustrations that could attend the drilling of a wildcat. Slick assumed the responsibility of completing the well, known as the Isabella test, after the original contractor died. No work had been done on the test for over a year when Slick took over and resumed drilling in May 1926. As usual, local boosters were enthusiastic: "Mr. Slick is considered one of the luckiest wildcatters in the state and everybody is hoping that his good luck will prove out in this test and he will succeed in bringing the black gold fluid to the top of the ground with a gusher."[67]

Trouble with the well began almost immediately. A water shortage hampered progress at first. Slick then paid for a water line to pump water from the Cimarron River. Once workers began pumping, rainfall came and filled the slush ponds. Then in late August two joints of drill pipe collapsed inside the well. When the driller attempted to pull the string of pipe from the hole, the pipe broke. This forced another delay while they awaited the arrival of special tools and pipe to correct the problem.[68] After drilling finally resumed, one of the workers had his jaw broken in an accident caused by a piece of drilling equipment. Work continued again with the hiring of a new employee. Then in December one of the drilling tools broke off in the hole. After three weeks of effort they failed to retrieve the tool and thus decided to drill through it. One month later, they abandoned the well as a dry hole.[69]

Fortunately for Slick, he had the money to survive this kind of disastrous venture. He also possessed the understanding that this was simply one unfortunate aspect or risk of the business. He clearly demonstrated this in his frustrating years before the Wheeler strike, and he continued to see failures as part of "the oil game." Slick also recognized that few people had the fortitude to succeed in this business. A journalist once asked Slick if he would advise a young man to embark on a career as a wildcatter. Slick replied, "No, I wouldn't. There are too many chances against him, and not one man in a million is built so he can take one knockout after another and still dig in without losing his pep. . . . It costs $65,000 to $75,000 and up to $100,000 to drill a well these days. One I drilled recently cost me $175,000. If he hits a duster he's busted, flat. So it's largely a gamble. Then he must have nerve to go on."[70]

In late 1926 Slick was ready for a rest from his interstate oil business, so he sold virtually all of his holdings in piecemeal fashion. Many oilmen did not even know Slick had taken a brief respite because he sold his holdings in unpublicized sales. He accomplished this by forming a corporation named Tom Slick, Inc., which held all of his oil properties with the exception of those in the Seminole area.[71] Slick then sold various properties to Prairie Oil and Gas over the next several months. The cumulative sale price revealed just how expansive his operations had become. He reputedly sold out for between fifteen and twenty million dollars.[72] Whether Slick sold his holdings purely for reasons of declining health or merely to raise capital for his next foray, a common tactic for many independents, cannot be positively determined.[73] It was likely that in Slick's case these purposes coincided.

Another reason many oilmen did not know of Slick's sellout was that he reentered the business after only a few months of vacation. Slick spent most of the time traveling with his family, making visits to his home in Clarion and to a newly purchased winter home in San Antonio, Texas. He soon returned to participate in developing one of the larger oil areas ever found in the United States—the Greater Seminole Field.

6

"Seminole Is the Greatest Pool of Oil Ever Discovered"

What we are headed for is some sort of governmental regulation. Our actions past and present are evidence we can not control conditions ourselves. Personally I would be glad if something could be done. But it looks like a hopeless effort now. We could make no progress when there were fewer companies and fewer wells. Conditions in the field are worse now and our attitude is no different. It would have been better for the industry if Seminole had never been discovered.

E. H. Moore, Independent Oil and Gas

The discovery and development of the Greater Seminole oil field lasted from 1923 to 1935. This area, encompassing virtually all of Seminole County, eastern Pottawatomie, and smaller portions of Hughes and Okfuskee Counties, emerged as one of the largest-producing oil fields in the world. Its massive production brought a staggering decline in the price of crude, which plummeted to fifteen cents per barrel. This situation forced operators to search for means to reduce production and raise prices. Oilmen also became aware

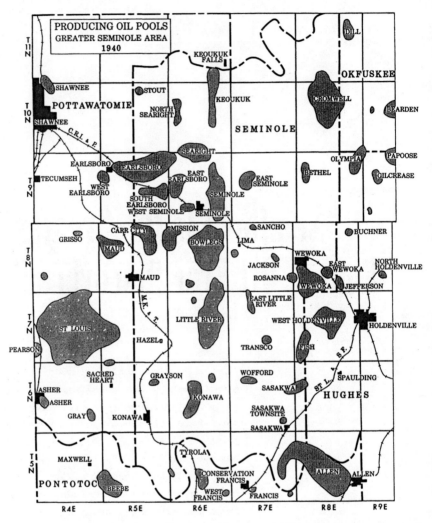

From Welsh, Townes, and Morris, History of the Greater Seminole Oil Field. *Courtesy Oklahoma Heritage Association*

that the boom mentality that encouraged them to drill as many wells as possible so that they could surpass or at least keep pace with the competition was wasteful. These practices squandered oil by putting far more on the market than consumers required. It also meant that operators drilled many more wells than were necessary for efficient production. The development of Seminole highlighted these various problems and forced the oil industry to seek solutions. Seminole marked the beginning of sincere efforts by many oilmen to rationalize the development of oil fields in order to protect a vital natural resource and to maximize their own economic gain. Tom Slick, an early convert to many conservation measures, found himself in a leadership role as others both sought and acted upon his advice.

Sustained efforts to find oil in Seminole County began in 1922. By April 1923 Slick entered the action when he purchased a well and its surrounding acreage from Kawfield Oil Company. Kawfield had begun the wildcat well in January 1923 but had experienced several setbacks. To avoid further losses, they sold the location to Slick.[1] He then renewed drilling on the Mingo No. 1, as the test was known, located about fifteen miles south of Wewoka. In the meantime Slick bought leases elsewhere in Seminole County, mainly in the Wewoka area.[2] In addition to acquiring acreage, the oilman backed the establishment of a lumberyard in Wewoka, where the Slick Lumber Company, a subsidiary of the Slick Townsite Company, purchased land.[3]

In December the Mingo No. 1 came in as a tremendous gas well, rated at over 5,000,000 cubic feet. The discovery attracted attention as oil operators began purchasing acreage throughout the area, but most continued to focus on the intense events surrounding the development of the pools at Wewoka and Cromwell.[4] Slick drilled at other scattered locations in the area, convinced that he would tap a large pool of oil somewhere in southern Seminole County.[5] But his operations in Tonkawa, Papoose, and at Cross Plains, Texas, engaged most of his attention. He also had drilling ventures in Kansas and in northern Mississippi.[6] Not until 1926, after he sold most of his other holdings, did Slick fully direct his energies to developing his properties in the Seminole area.

Slick enjoyed success in most of the pools that comprised the Seminole field. Two of his leases and the manner by which he acquired them exemplified his business practices and the unusual good fortune that generally resulted from his efforts. The first important deal involved a lease two miles southeast of the town of Seminole. A business associate of Slick said that he "saw Slick meet a man on the street and, standing there, he contracted to pay $100,000 for an oil lease . . . in the heart of the Seminole field. Slick asked simply: 'What do you want for that lease?' 'A hundred·thousand dollars,' replied the owner. 'It's a sale, bring in your deeds,' said Slick."[7] With little more ceremony than this, the oilman began drilling the Franks No. 1, which, by January 1927, operators declared was "the banner well of the Seminole field."[8] The well gushed in during mid-November at a rate of 5,000 barrels per day. Over the next months the production from the well increased. In December its flow had improved to 7,500 barrels. The following month production swelled to 9,984 barrels. After only five months the Franks No. 1 had produced 1,000,000 barrels of high gravity crude, which sold for about $2.20 per barrel.[9]

Slick's second major Seminole deal was made in much the same fashion and had similar results. This deal involved the Hembree lease on the eastern edge of the Saint Louis pool. Bill James, the oilman who sold the lease to Slick, related the details of the simple transaction. "I met [Slick] one day and he, knowing that I was leasing some land, asked me: 'Well, Bill, what you got?' I told him I had for sale the 40-acre [Hembree] lease in Pottawatomie County. 'What do you want for it?' he asked. 'Two thousand dollars,' I answered." Slick replied, "I'll take it."[10] In June 1928 he completed a well on the lease rated at more than 9,000 barrels daily. This well tapped the rich Wilcox sand, and its abundant flow encouraged other operators in the pool to deepen their wells.[11]

From 1926 to 1928 oilmen found that the Greater Seminole field was comprised of several major pools of oil. These included Earlsboro, Saint Louis, Seminole City, Searight, Cromwell, Wewoka, Mission, Maud, Little River, and Bowlegs. Development of the field was a great episode in Oklahoma's history, which impacted the local, state, and even national economies. But the massive output from this field and its hasty development aggravated the oil industry's problems—overproduction, low prices, overdrilling, and both physical and economic waste. At this critical time, calls for solutions emerged. Leaders of the industry made several attempts at self-regulation, but these early efforts met only modest success. However, they did pave the way for the permanent measures that came after Slick's death in 1930.

Many of the difficulties that the oil industry faced centered on a basic premise that oilmen and courts called the rule of capture. This common-law rule held that landowners (or lessees) owned all that was produced from wells on their land regardless of the source of supply. The Pennsylvania Supreme Court in 1889 ruled that oil and gas, "In common with animals, and unlike other minerals, [has] the power and the tendency to escape without the volition of the owner. . . . They belong to the owner of the land and are part of it, so long as they are on it or in it, and are subject to his control; but when they escape and go into other land, or come under another's control, the title of the former owner is gone."[12] With this understanding, operators drilled their first wells near property lines so as to drain much of the oil from their neighbor's land. Then they might drill additional wells at various other points on their property to finish draining the pool of oil. Wells drilled near the property line meant that the adjacent landowner had to drill an offset well in order to protect his property rights. This forced producers to drill numerous wells as quickly as possible in order to secure a larger share of the oil. Even if the oil could not be sold or transported to a market, the operators had to produce the oil to prevent a neighbor from draining his share. Such activities resulted in flagrant waste of oil and gas and prompted passage of the first conservation laws.[13]

Oklahoma led the way in early conservation legislation, particularly in a statute that provided a broad definition of waste and clearly empowered the state corporation commission to deal with this matter. The 1915 law stated, "The term 'waste' as used herein, in addition to its ordinary meaning, shall include economic waste, underground waste, surface waste, and waste incident to the production of crude oil [and natural gas] . . . in excess of transportation or marketing facilities or reasonable market demands. The corporation commission shall have authority to make rules and regulations for the prevention of such wastes."[14] Over the next ten years the state corporation commission devised various rules and imposed its controls on the state's oil industry with measures such as requiring drilling permits, well logs, and well completion records.[15] But the tremendous demand for oil in World War I, and in the years immediately following when the automobile flourished, kept prices relatively high and complaints by operators at a minimum.

By 1926 Seminole began its rise to preeminence in oil production. At this critical point the corporation commission, for three reasons, hesitated to act in curtailing production. First, the commission had failed to enforce some of its rulings in the previous years, thus impairing its authority. Second, the commission lacked personnel and funding to supervise developments in the large Seminole field. And third, they seemed timid when facing the opposition of oilmen who rejected the idea of government intervention.[16] Slick spoke for many oilmen when he stated, "I have always felt that the less government interference had in business, the better it would be. At the same time I realize that when a man becomes insane that the best way to conserve his property is to appoint a guardian at once. In such a case if the man regains his faculties, the guardian is released and he again takes charge of his properties; but in the case of the oil industry if the government is appointed guardian, regardless of how sane the industry becomes, we will always have the guardian."[17] This fear of government intrusion led Seminole operators to attempt numerous means of cooperation and self-regulation as they groped for a fair means of reducing production, raising prices, and conserving oil.

The first attempt at curtailing oil output was through the use of proration. This technique had been used in previous boom periods, at Cushing and Healdton, for example. In this case, however, operators were asked voluntarily to cooperate in an effort to reduce production by 10 percent. The Seminole producers hired Ray M. Collins to serve as umpire and supervise the curtailment. The umpire had the formidable task of gathering data on the production and consumption of oil. He then adjusted the amount that all operators produced to correspond with market demands. This meant that producers had to reduce proportionally, or prorate, the amount of oil from their wells. Operators accomplished this by "pinching down," or restricting the flow from each well. Collins called several meetings of the Seminole producers in an attempt to devise proration plans. But they failed to find a method of curtailing production that proved acceptable to all.

Slick did not always attend these meetings. However, he was present at a July 1927 gathering where members grudgingly asked the corporation commission to take action in devising and enforcing a plan of curtailment.[18] Of the forty-one companies with interests in Seminole, only thirty-one sent representatives to the meeting, and of these, fifteen refused to vote. Ten gave their approval, and six voted against the resolution, hardly a mandate for reform.[19] The measure called for cooperation between the corporation commission and an owners' group, known as the Seminole Advisory Committee, which would establish a proration plan.

While Slick voted in favor of this resolution, his actions and comments during the next three years revealed his ambivalence. When asked to join a curtailment agreement with producers in the Saint Louis pool, Slick flatly refused, stating, "I do not think proration fair and I will not join with you."[20] Shortly after making this comment Slick appeared before the corporation commission, which was hearing testimony concerning the benefit and equity of proration. He testified that by choking or pinching the flow from a large well the owner ran the risk of damaging it. He argued instead that operators should be allowed to prorate their wells located in settled fields. Slick pointed out that the flow from these older wells could be more easily regulated, and without the risk of damaging the well.[21]

Slick also earned the gratitude of the smaller operators when he insisted that prorating only one field hurt their business. His point was that larger oil firms usually owned properties in several fields while smaller ones tended to own wells only in active oil areas. Thus, larger firms could absorb losses resulting from proration because they maintained production elsewhere. Smaller operators lacked this advantage.[22] To remedy this inequity, Slick suggested a total shutdown of the state oil fields for one day each week. He offered Sunday as the most logical day. Slick made this proposal in early 1928, and most accounts agreed that this idea originated with him.[23] In an appearance before the corporation commission, he declared that "if any pinching down is going to be done, all the wells in Oklahoma will be pinched down for 24 hours, say—on Sunday so the field men can have a rest."[24]

The oil industry failed to act upon Slick's proposal until Sunday, February 17, 1929, when the Barnsdall Oil Company announced that it would adopt the plan, but only for its Seminole holdings. Two days later Slick agreed to do so, and the following day Prairie Oil and Gas decided to join. Others, including Sinclair, Phillips, Magnolia, ITIO, and Pure, agreed to comply shortly thereafter. Over the next several months the shutdown arrangement reduced production by an average of 80,000 barrels for each Sunday.[25] Although the nationwide effect was minimal, it demonstrated that oilmen could cooperate to reduce production.

Slick also believed that proration had other shortcomings. His chief complaint was that it violated the discovery rights of an operator who was forced to curtail his production while others were allowed to continue drilling. In one angry outburst concerning this issue, Slick exclaimed, "You want me to pinch down my wells until you can get a chance to get yours dug so that you can take some of my oil. And you can't do it!"[26] He felt that the discoverer and the first producers in a new area should be allowed to take a greater share of the oil as compensation for their efforts. A related issue, but one with even wider implications, concerned the fact that while Oklahoma producers might prorate their wells, producers in other states and nations had no such restraints. In October 1928 Slick complained that since Oklahoma crude production had been reduced, one refiner wanted "to run the heavy West Texas oil through their lines to meet the demand for fuel oil. Proration as we have it is unfair."[27] This matter, however, required interstate cooperation and was not resolved until several years later.

Another aspect of proration that Slick disliked was that it seemed to benefit refiners to a greater degree than producers. He argued that refiners had kept gasoline prices high while paying greatly reduced prices for crude.[28] Closely related to this complaint was Slick's belief that the composition of the Seminole Advisory Committee was unrepresentative. At an October 1928 meeting of Seminole producers he charged that a "committee of refiners and three state officials who admittedly know nothing about the oil business are trying to run a $6,000,000,000 industry in Oklahoma."[29] Four days later the committee added three independent oilmen as members.

By 1929 Slick had adopted a more favorable view toward proration. This may have been because there was some consideration by oilmen and the corporation commission that proration should be applied on a statewide basis rather than restricting a single field. Also, Kansas operators seemed to be in general sympathy with these efforts. Slick himself had steadily endorsed cooperation among oilmen as the best means for finding solutions to the oil crisis, and he may have believed that his fight against certain aspects of proration was incongruous with his calls for harmony. Whatever the reason, Slick consented to abide by a February 1929 proration agreement for Seminole.

Later that year he suggested a plan for the Oklahoma City field, which operators implemented. This arrangement divided wells into two groups and scheduled days on which they could produce at full capacity. All wells, however, ceased production on Sundays.[30] Another sign of his acceptance of proration could be found in the fact that he agreed to serve on a special committee for the American Petroleum Institute, which tried to devise curtailment strategies.[31]

In addition to his evolving acceptance of proration, Slick consistently decried the wasteful, inefficient, and unprofitable practices by which oil companies currently operated. Slick believed that "Seminole is the greatest pool of oil ever discovered. It should have made millions of dollars for the producers interested. Instead of that, I feel the oil fraternity has lost a hundred million or more."[32] He complained that current leasing practices led to the acquisition of small, scattered tracts of land. When an operator discovered oil, all lease owners had to respond immediately by drilling their own wells. "You then have a big field under way," Slick stated, and "you might just as well try to stop a cyclone as try to stop the big field that is under way."[33]

To slow down this boom Slick suggested that companies only buy leases in 160-acre tracts: "In the future I think the large companies and large producers should do everything in their power to eliminate the 10-acre leases, the 5-acre leases, the school lots, the 40-acre lease and the 80-acre leases." Instead, oil companies "should purchase only 160-acre leases around wildcat wells and they should have a contract with all the purchasers and the man that drills the well, as to how this property is to be operated after production is found."[34] By consolidating the leases and rationalizing the development, "there would never be any great rush, the roads would not be congested as at Seminole, they would save millions of dollars in pipelines which would be taken up in the course of six months or a year—and, further, when you come to the edge of the pool the oil fraternity would possibly drill two or three dry holes, while under the present method, as in parts of Seminole County, there will be 25 to 50 dry holes drilled, where two or three would condemn the territory."[35]

Therefore, Slick believed oil producers could help reduce the waste associated with overproduction and overdrilling by using the relatively new techniques known as unitization and well spacing. Unitization referred to consolidating "a number of separately owned properties [leases] into one large property to be developed and operated as such at the proportional expense and for the proportional benefit of the several parties in interest."[36] By treating the entire pool as a unit of production, rather than each lease, the controlled development would greatly reduce both economic and physical waste. Drilling fewer wells would aid this process. With proper well spacing, the minimum number of wells would be drilled so as to drain the pool in the most efficient manner and allow the maximum recovery of oil. All property owners would still benefit, even if they did not have wells on their land, since profits were distributed proportionally.[37]

Unitization and well spacing presented an obvious challenge to the rule of capture concept. When Henry L. Doherty, founder of Cities Service Company, first attempted to explain his proposal of unitization at a 1924 meeting of the American Petroleum Institute, the directors of that body refused to let him speak. But the logic and value of his ideas slowly gained acceptance after 1925 when Doherty made his views known at a presentation before the American Institute of Mining and Metallurgical Engineers.[38] Oilmen soon witnessed the change in perceptions. Legislatures and courts sanctioned it. In 1932 the Oklahoma Supreme Court expressed this fundamental shift in thought when it ruled, "Surface owners of land have the right to drill for and reduce to possession the oil and gas beneath; but this right is to all owners alike; and when numerous surface owners seek to produce from a common pool, it is within the police power of the state, in keeping with due process of law, to require the several surface owners to produce same under reasonable regulations to the end that some of said owners may not take from the common source more than their equitable share."[39] By treating the pool as a natural entity, unitization served as an extension of the principle of correlative rights that governed the use of surface waters as a common resource to riparian owners.

Slick accepted unitization and well spacing as solutions to the dual problems of overproduction and overdrilling. In 1927 Slick and Edwin B. Reeser, president of the Barnsdall Oil Company, initiated one of the first attempts to unitize a prospective oil pool. This effort began when a wildcat well that Slick drilled erupted as a huge gusher in June 1927. The Walker No. 1, about seven miles north of Ada in Pontotoc County, Oklahoma, spurted oil about 120 feet into the air at the rate of 5,000 barrels daily.[40] The well had found a prolific, but unexpected, oil sand that many guessed might be an extension of the Greater Seminole field located just a few miles north of the well.

The discovery attracted the usual rush of visitors and speculators to the area. Within one day entrepreneurs, those looking for work, and prospective residents crowded the area around the well and established a new boomtown—Slicker City, the third such town to be named after Slick.[41] Sleeping on cots scattered among the trees, or in tents in the case of the more fortunate, they cleared lots, laid out streets, and announced plans for a variety of businesses, including cafes and a lumberyard. All of these efforts were made in anticipation of the expected boom for the ragtown.[42]

Meanwhile, Reeser and Slick held a meeting of the leaseholders who had acreage around the well. The concerned oil companies decided to combine their total leases and operate them as a single unit. To accomplish this they formed a new enterprise, the Conservation Oil Company, and pooled their acreage under its control: Tom Slick, 450 acres; Barnsdall, 320; Atlantic, 160; Margay, 120; Tidal, 120; Mid-Continent, 80; and Sinclair, 80.[43] Each would bear a proportion of the drilling expenses and receive a proportion of the profits. Reeser stated that "the policy of the new company will be one of strict conservation, applying this policy to [the] rate of development with reference to economic considerations as well as to conservation of gas pressure and scientific development of the whole property."[44]

Unfortunately, the experiment in unitization was about as short-lived as the boomtown of Slicker City. Subsequent drilling failed to yield oil, but the Walker No. 1 produced approximately one million barrels for Slick and the other associates of Conservation Oil.[45] Nevertheless, the experiment had one important result. It offered proof that oilmen could cooperate. It was this spirit that Slick hoped to foster as he advocated unitization and well spacing as conservation measures.

To this end, Slick made an uncharacteristic appearance before a group of industry leaders at the Petroleum Exposition in Tulsa in October 1927. This annual event brought together producers and others associated with the oil industry from around the world. Visitors could view exhibits of oil field machinery and equipment in what was much like a World's Fair for the oil industry.[46] Slick addressed this assembly expressing support for the conservation measures that he was currently employing with Conservation Oil. He warned that failure by the oil fraternity to cooperate in the various private efforts to solve the industry's problems would result in government intervention. Slick made these comments at a time when Seminole operators sought solutions to the chronic problem of overproduction. In his oration Slick offered several suggestions for improvement. He believed that all companies should purchase leases in 160-acre blocks or at least consolidate smaller blocks into larger units. He strongly advocated drilling only five wells on each 160-acre unit—one in the center of each forty acres and one in the center of the entire block. Slick went on to say, "Regardless of how you space your wells, I feel that it is absolutely necessary for the producers to get together and arrange so there will be no more than one string of drilling tools operating on 160 acres at any one time."[47]

To convince those who had lingering doubts about using these techniques,

*Slick's Walker No. 1, near Ada, Oklahoma. Courtesy
Western History Collections, University of Oklahoma Library*

Slick hosted a banquet at the Tulsa Country Club on January 17, 1928. He invited leaders of the oil industry from Oklahoma, Kansas, Texas, and New York to attend. Slick believed the gathering would enable the leaders to become better acquainted and allow them to exchange ideas in a friendly setting. In addition to these reasons, Slick noted, "I have called the men together at this dinner because I seemed to be the logical one to do it, for I don't believe I have an enemy among either the big producers or the little ones, and I have the kindliest feeling toward them all."[48]

Only three months after giving his first public speech, Slick gave his second when he delivered the keynote address to his guests. On this occasion he refined many of the points made in his previous remarks at the Petroleum Exposition. Slick told the two hundred guests in attendance that cooperation would be the key to success in solving their problems. One new idea that he advocated in this speech concerned the establishment of a committee comprised of delegates from all companies willing to participate. These members would be empowered to make immediate decisions for their company in agreeing to conservation plans. Slick warned that unless oilmen took bold measures, they would be condemned to repeating the losses and waste experienced in past oil booms: "Every major pool in Oklahoma has brought the price of oil down to a point where there was no profit in it. This was true in the Glenn Pool, Cushing, Tonkawa, Burbank—all of them. This is wholly unnecessary. Drilling in all such pools should be carried on under some conservative and common-sense agreement that would not require sacrifice of profits and needless production of oil."[49]

Slick continued to participate in other unitized drilling agreements, proving the sincerity of his interest in this conservation technique. The most prominent example was southeast of the Searight pool in Seminole County. Slick, Carter, ITIO, Continental, Sinclair, Houston, McMan, and Amerada pooled their leases into a block of 640 acres.[50] According to figures compiled by the Mid-Continent Oil and Gas Association (MCO&GA), this experiment in unitization was successful. The group drilled only fifteen wells—fourteen producers and one dry hole. The MCO&GA calculated that if the pool had not been unitized, thirty-two wells would have been drilled: twenty-four producers and eight dry. Thus, by unitizing the pool, the participants saved the waste, expense, and excess production of seventeen wells while still efficiently draining the pool.[51]

Slick entered two other unitization agreements shortly before his death in 1930. One involved an extensive tract of 2,560 acres in Noble County, Oklahoma. He pooled his acreage with Gypsy, Prairie, Magnolia, Sinclair, Wentz, Mid-Continent, Texas, and Comar. The other tract was west of the

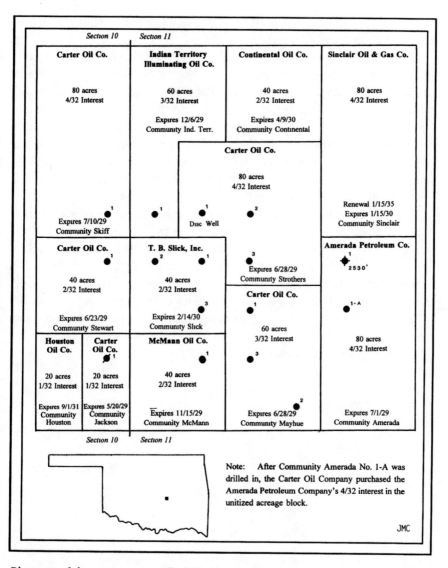

Plat map of the community wells drilled in the Searight pool (sections 10 and 11 of township 9 north, range 6 east, Seminole County, Oklahoma), an early unitization project by Slick, Carter Oil, ITIO, and others.
After map MCO&GA, Unitization

Chandler pool in Lincoln County, Oklahoma. Here Slick combined his acreage with Prairie and Magnolia.[52]

From 1927 to 1930 Slick participated in the emerging conservation movement in the petroleum industry. The vast output of Seminole forced the industry to deal with the chronic problem of overproduction. Slick only mildly endorsed the idea of proration. For unitization and well-spacing he gave enthusiastic support and participated in several unitization experiments. However, the culmination of these early conservation measures was not reached until 1935, five years after Slick's death, with the establishment of the Interstate Oil Compact Commission. This agency coordinated the various state efforts as each member state passed conservation legislation.

During the years of flush production at Seminole and the search for effective conservation measures, Slick had expanded his interests beyond the Greater Seminole area. He had assembled a large block of leases south of Coyle in Logan County, Oklahoma, that covered about 7,000 acres. He drilled a well near the town of Coyle which produced only a small amount of oil. Slick later drilled two other wells on the block of land but failed to find oil.[53] The oilman also acquired holdings in Kansas and Texas, but developments southeast of Oklahoma City attracted his attention by 1929. It was here that Slick made his final plunge in the oil business.

"Within a Year, I'll Be Back on Top"

A wildcatter can't quit, no matter how enormous the odds against him. The oil's there waiting, but it won't show itself unless you seek it, and seek it strenuously.

Mike Benedum

As of 1929 Slick had enjoyed tremendous success in Oklahoma, Kansas, and Texas oil fields. Oilmen, journalists, editors, leaders of the Oklahoma oil industry, and the public generally regarded Slick as the largest independent oil operator in the nation. He earned a reputation as an honest, decisive, and shrewd businessman. With certain reservations, Slick had shown himself to be a leading advocate of the nascent conservation movement. State officials and other oilmen sought and implemented his ideas and suggestions. It came, therefore, as a surprise when in March 1929 newspapers announced that Slick would sell his holdings and retire.

Part of his consideration regarding retirement must have included his declining health. Since 1927 he had devoted much of his personal time to developing his holdings in the Seminole field. In one well-publicized account Slick slept five nights on the "pine board" floor of the boiler room at one of his rigs. He insisted on supervising the drilling progress there and refused to leave.[1] Slick spent much time at all of his Seminole leases, probably because of the area's proximity to his residence in Oklahoma City. While such actions endeared him to his lessors and employees, it failed to contribute to his general health. In early 1929 Slick's wife and family pleaded with him to sell his holdings and take an extensive vacation. Slick reluctantly agreed.[2]

Many journalists characterized the sale of Slick's properties to Prairie Oil and Gas Company as the largest transfer ever made by an independent oilman. Officials representing Slick and Prairie concluded the arrangements in mid-March 1929. Slick sold his entire daily production, estimated at between 30,000 and 35,000 barrels. In addition he sold all of his oil in storage, tankage, drilling equipment, and one-half interest in all of his undeveloped acreage, estimated at more than 500,000 acres. Slick, however, maintained full ownership of all royalties.[3] The principals never revealed the exact price paid. Prairie officials would not be more specific than to say the price was "between $10,000,000 and $100,000,000."[4] Most oilmen and journalists believed the price Prairie paid was approximately $35,000,000. This figure was probably reasonable considering the offers that Slick refused— $28,000,000 from Standard Oil of Indiana, $30,000,000 from Standard Oil of New Jersey, and $32,000,000 from Standard Oil of New York.[5]

Prairie's purchase vaulted the company into the ranks of the nation's leading oil producers, as its daily production increased to more than 100,000 barrels. Much of the crude gained from the deal with Slick would be transported through Prairie's existing pipeline network. In addition, Prairie now owned an interest in Slick's wildcat acreage. This greatly enhanced its prospects for future production.[6]

The sale to Prairie focused a great deal of attention on Slick. Newspapers throughout the Mid-Continent area carried articles concerning the $35,000,000 deal. Interest in Slick after the sale led a reporter for the *Kansas City Star* to seek an interview with him. Slick granted that newspaper the only interview he ever gave. Other papers and oil journals also printed stories about Slick.[7] All noted that he seemed tired and would, in all probability, take an extended vacation or perhaps retire. But Slick left the issue of his retirement open: "Just say I'm not through with the oil business." Others quoted Slick as betting his associates that "within a year, I'll be back on top as the world's biggest individual oil producer."[8]

Soon after the sale, Slick presented his two closest friends, Charles Urschel and E. E. Kirkpatrick, with a token of his appreciation for their assistance in conducting the negotiations with Prairie. Slick, in an astounding gesture of generosity, gave each of them a check for $2,000,000.[9] Kirkpatrick expressed his gratitude several months later at Christmas in a letter to Slick. Using cowboy vernacular in a humorous and somewhat prophetic letter, Kirkpatrick wrote:

> Dear Tom,
>
> Christmas times when a fellow feels thankful for a lot o' things there shore ain't nothin' I kin say to show my appreciashun of what you've done for me.
>
> Back in '23 when I rode my horse into yore remuda, I just figgered as how it would be another hard winter with a few wages and eats, but when you cut me in for an interest in the herd and we finally sold the outfit for all the money in the till and I can have whatever cow ponies and saddles and boots I want, my heart's shore filled to overflowin' with gratitude to you.
>
> I allows as how I ain't got nothin' much to do the balance o' my life but just ride herd on yore troubles, and if any loplegged hombre comes fence cuttin' or throwin' stray brands on any o' yore calves, why I'll start shootin' suddin'.
>
> And Tom, on the long ride through distant ranges, if you should cross the rim rock and go down the long trail ahead o' me to the big round-up, why I'll shore keep up the fences and stand guard on the outfit and see that no rustler breaks into yore cattle.
>
> I'm hopin' you have a good Christmas and I'm thankin' you agin for fixin' it so I'll always have plenty o' sowbelly and beans.
>
> Yore's truly,
Kirk.[10]

Slick's "extended vacation" lasted only two weeks after the Prairie sale. Within this short period of time he made preparations for what proved to be his final plunge into the oil business. Yet he made these plans with a view toward reducing his own role in managing his oil properties. Slick wanted to organize three separate companies that would develop and expand his operations in Kansas, Texas, and Oklahoma. One of Slick's trusted associates would head each company, thus relieving the oilman from the burden of routine supervision. However, Slick remained in ultimate control. In March and April of 1929, he implemented these arrangements to a limited degree.[11]

To handle his proposed expansion into Kansas, Slick acquired two partners, Ralph Pryor and Floyd Lockhart, the owners of the Pryor and Lockhart Oil Company based in Wichita, Kansas. Ralph Pryor, a graduate of the University of Kansas, spent several years selling life insurance and automobiles in Dodge City.[12] Floyd Lockhart, a University of Michigan graduate, likewise spent some time as a car salesman and later worked as a geologist for the Marland Oil Company. In 1918 the two men met in Wichita and entered the oil business as partners. Pryor used his salesmanship and business talents while Lockhart contributed his knowledge of geology and the oil industry. Together they enjoyed success in the El Dorado field of Kansas and at Borger, Texas, but confined most of their operations to Kansas.[13]

Slick met Pryor and Lockhart in late 1928 through a business deal arranged by Slick's former associate at Tonkawa, Henry Rosenthal. Pryor and Lockhart and Aladdin Petroleum (of which Rosenthal was a major stockholder) owned a block of four hundred acres near the Wright oil pool north of Wichita. As that pool developed, the lease became more valuable. Rosenthal thought Slick might be interested in drilling a well. Slick agreed. He bought one-half interest in the lease from Pryor and Rosenthal.[14]

Drilling commenced on the new well in November 1928 and progressed rapidly. In late December as the well neared completion, Slick traveled to Kansas to witness the event. An employee of Aladdin Petroleum noted that Slick stayed at the rig all day watching the work from a seat on an apple crate and noted his great excitement when the well came in as a gusher.[15] Based on this success, Slick ordered the drilling of three new wells. At this point Slick bought the remaining interest held by Aladdin for about $350,000. This time fortune sided with Rosenthal as one month later all three wells came in dry and the first well stopped producing.[16]

Despite this failure Slick continued his association with Ralph Pryor and Floyd Lockhart. In March 1929 Slick purchased Pryor and Lockhart Oil for one million dollars. The deal included forty thousand acres of leases and some valuable oil properties at Valley Center, Kansas. He then formed a new company, Slick, Pryor, and Lockhart, Inc. (SP&L) to develop and expand his newly acquired holdings in addition to his wildcat acreage in Kansas.[17] SP&L best exemplified Slick's goal of reducing his personal role in conducting his business operations.

Pryor and Lockhart handled Slick's Kansas business from offices based in Wichita, as the new partners enjoyed immense success developing acreage throughout that state. Their first efforts came in Russell County, about fifteen miles southeast of the town of Russell. Slick took over a block of leases from E. W. Marland, who four years earlier had drilled a well there with some signs of oil. Despite this, Marland elected not to renew the leases and sold them to Slick. The locals were highly optimistic: "If T. B. Slick's reputation stands up to advance information his test on the Sellens [lease] will be a producer. Mr. Slick is known as the lucky driller and an oil man . . . recently said that he picked up blocks that others had dropped and when he drilled, oil came to the surface."[18] Three months after SP&L began drilling, the Sellens No. 1 came in as a good producer. This well proved to be the discovery well of what eventually developed into the Trapp field. This new oil field covered several square miles and straddled the center of the border between Russell and Barton Counties.[19]

SP&L next moved thirty miles southeast near the town of Raymond in Rice County. Here Slick completed an unusual business deal in which he actually purchased a discovery well. Slick paid $250,000 for the Schurr No. 1 and 2,000 acres of leases. This well produced an exceptionally rich grade of oil, rated at fifty-five gravity.[20] Once again, local citizens grew excited at the prospect that Slick would be developing the acreage: "The Raymond community seems elated at the thought that Mr. Slick has bought the Schurr well. . . . Knowing of his successful pursuits for many years, especially in wildcat holes, they feel more certain than ever that the Schurr is opening a new field for Rice County in their community."[21] SP&L drilled several more wells in the area, which produced in even greater quantities than the Schurr No. 1. Many other operators moved into western Rice County as well and helped develop what became one of the largest fields in central Kansas, the Chase-Silica field. Years later, writers credited SP&L with discovering the field, without realizing that Slick had purchased the well after its completion.[22]

SP&L met success in drilling ventures scattered elsewhere in Kansas. Their Grattan No. 1, just south of McPherson, Kansas, helped extend the Voshell pool northward as the well located a new pay sand and produced about six hundred barrels per day.[23] Their Peasel No. 1 was the discovery well for the Wellington pool in northern Sumner County. They completed this well, located between the towns of Wellington and Conway Springs, in December 1929 as an average producer.[24]

Pryor and Lockhart continued to operate SP&L after Slick's death in August 1930. Both were highly competent oilmen who enjoyed success in the subsequent years, discovering three oil pools in Barton, Ellsworth, and Rice Counties. In November 1936 SP&L still had forty-five producing wells with an aggregate production of 16,965 barrels daily.[25] The following year Charles Urschel, the executor of Slick's estate, dissolved SP&L.[26]

Slick never completed his plans for a company based in Fort.Worth to manage his Texas interests. Since he had far fewer holdings in that state Slick chose to operate there by financing drilling ventures that seemed promising. One company that he backed was SRC Oil of San Antonio. Slick's brother-in-law Arthur A. Seeligson and his partners Earnest B. Rubsamen, Jr., and Charles P. Cartter, operated SRC and developed most of Slick's south Texas acreage in 1929 and 1930.[27] Slick played a limited role in his Texas operations, focusing almost exclusively on his properties in Oklahoma and Kansas.

Tom Slick's holdings in south Texas were widely scattered in DeWitt,

Bee, Goliad, Duvall, Starr, Zapata, and Young Counties. Most of the production that resulted from Slick and SRC drilling in late 1929 and 1930 tended to be rather small when compared to the wells of Oklahoma City. Their greatest success came in Zapata County, where they drilled on the Cuellar ranch, and on the border of DeWitt and Goliad Counties. Here the partners discovered a new oil pool, which they named in honor of Slick. SRC completed the well in December 1930, almost four months after Slick's death.[28]

One month after his sellout to Prairie and shortly after the formation of SP&L, Slick formed a new corporation to conduct his Oklahoma oil business. On April 15, 1929, he chartered the Tom Slick Oil Company with himself as the president. Charles F. Urschel served as the treasurer and first vice president, while Ernest E. Kirkpatrick became the second vice president. J. H. Grant, a longtime friend of Slick, served as secretary. In the proposed scheme of operation Kirkpatrick would manage all drilling, leasing, and production from an office in Tulsa. Urschel would be responsible for all financing and accounting and would work at his office in Oklahoma City. Slick, meanwhile, would be the nominal head of the company overseeing its general operation, having ample time to travel and spend with his family.[29] But instead of fully implementing his plan and taking vacation time, he resumed working as intensely as ever.

One of Slick's first big moves after his sale to Prairie was near the small town of Asher in southern Pottawatomie County, Oklahoma. Interest in the area increased in April 1929 when Simms Petroleum Company completed a large producer. Shortly thereafter Slick purchased much of the surrounding acreage from his former partner, Charles J. Wrightsman, for $1,200,000. For this price Slick obtained the leases on 350 acres.[30] A drilling campaign for the pay sand commenced at once. Slick owned ten of the twenty wells begun in the area. The drillers made rapid progress, and after about one month oil began to flow.[31] Slick, however, concentrated most of his attention on his efforts in the Oklahoma City area, leaving most of the work at Asher to Kirkpatrick.

Since 1903, promoters, oilmen, and various entrepreneurs had searched unsuccessfully for oil in Oklahoma County. By the 1920s geologists began mapping the area and offered favorable appraisals.[32] In 1925 John R. Bunn and Joe Cromwell began drilling a well north of the state capitol. The two men were in Tulsa when they received word urging them to return to Oklahoma City immediately. When they arrived they went directly to the well. Bunn remembered, "As we walked through the engine room to the rig floor, we passed a man in an old, beat-up leather jacket sitting on the lazy bench and puffing a big cigar."[33] Cromwell exclaimed, "There's that damn Tom

Slick, how the hell did he know what's going on?"[34] Bunn said they both "took heart because Slick either had a sixth sense or else contacts with drillers, for he always seemed to be at the right place at the right time as far as an oil discovery was concerned."[35] Slick acted upon the favorable signs from their well and began buying leases around the Oklahoma City area.

Soon after completion of the Cromwell and Bunn test, interest shifted southeast of the city to an area prospected by geologists working for the Indian Territory Illuminating Oil Company (ITIO). Based on favorable reports, the ITIO leased approximately ten thousand acres on a structure. This assured the company's dominance of the Oklahoma City field after their discovery well was completed in December 1928.[36] But other operators held important leases, Tom Slick among them. He controlled more than three hundred acres, just one-half mile east of the ITIO discovery well.

In 1929 the drilling campaign to develop the Oklahoma City field progressed rapidly. Over the next two years on virtually every lease that Slick owned, wells came in with massive production. This situation helped make him the largest independent operator in the field. In May 1930, for example, four of his new wells produced a total of 21,000 barrels of oil and 50,000,000 cubic feet of gas daily. His production figures for August climbed even higher when four more new wells flowed over 68,000 barrels per day.[37] Ironically, the largest well that Slick ever drilled came in one week after his death in August 1930. This Oklahoma City well, the Campbell No. 1, was rated at 43,200 barrels per day.[38]

Drilling wells in the Oklahoma City field presented several problems for operators. The massive production coupled with the onset of an economic depression made limitations on output imperative. Proration went into effect immediately as the field showed every sign of surpassing even the Greater Seminole field in potential production. Yet some oilmen faced financial difficulties and refused to abide by the state-imposed limitations on each well's output. Those operators who sold any oil in excess of their well's allowable amount were guilty of selling what was known as "hot oil." Oilmen and pipeline companies developed subterfuges to avoid detection in this illegal activity, and many considered the fact that prices remained depressed as the best proof that hot oil continued to flow from storage tanks.[39] Charles Mee, one of Slick's employees responsible for selling production to the pipeline companies, said that on several occasions he was asked to sell hot oil. Refusing to do so, Mee explained that Slick was one of the largest producers in the entire field. If he sold hot oil it would have an adverse effect on the price of crude.[40]

Higher costs presented another difficulty for those who wanted to drill in

Tom Slick examining an oil storage tank in the Oklahoma City field, circa 1929. Courtesy Western History Collections, University of Oklahoma Library

the Oklahoma City field. Rotary drilling had grown in popularity because wells could be completed more quickly, but this new technology was more expensive. The greater depth of the productive horizons at Oklahoma City contributed to the increased expense as well. Slick noted that most of the wells that he drilled in 1929 cost between $65,000 and $100,000. An official with ITIO compiled figures showing an average well depth of 6,500 feet at a cost of $155,000 for that company.[41]

Drilling near and in an urban area gave oilmen still more problems. They had to obtain special drilling permits and abide by applicable city codes. Operators faced numerous lawsuits for damages caused by spilled oil, exploding machinery, conflicting title claims, or wild wells. For these reasons, Tom Slick had more than sixty lawsuits filed against him from November 1929 to August 1930.[42] One of Slick's friends, Mood Hughes, went to lunch with Slick in 1930 and noted that "Slick was so nervous that he could hardly eat. He was much disturbed, as one of the big wells in the Oklahoma City field was out of control and spraying oil all over the country. Slick feared it might catch on fire and do a great deal of damage."[43] That well was the Sigmon No. 1, and Slick had almost twenty lawsuits filed against him, and against Prairie and Phillips Petroleum who co-owned the well, for damages.

Perhaps Slick's most notable wild well blew out of control shortly after his death and provided the first occasion for Governor William H. Murray to call out the National Guard. It was also the first wild well within the Oklahoma City limits. The Wepaco No. 1 roared out of control on the morning of January 19, 1931, spewing crude at the rate of 2,000 barrels hourly. The well threatened the city's business district and was only eight blocks east of city hall. Fearing the one spark that could ignite the well, the city fire chief ordered an immediate evacuation of the surrounding area. Officials halted all railroad traffic and requested that the governor send National Guard troops to help seal off the neighborhood. Murray responded by sending one hundred men to patrol approximately ten square blocks. By nightfall workers regained control of the well, and on the following day residents were allowed to return.[44]

Slick feared this type of damaging wild well and had expressed these concerns to his friend, Mood Hughes, in the summer of 1930. Hughes asked Slick why he did not retire and thus relieve himself of such anxiety. He replied, "I'm going to. I have a lot of work to do to clean up. I have more production than when I sold to the Prairie, and just as soon as I can get the loose ends together, I'm going to turn it over to them."[45] Slick had won his bet though. He had regained the title accorded to him by his peers and by the press as the largest independent operator in the nation. In the Oklahoma City field he owned choice leases and his wells comprised fourteen percent of all wells producing or being drilled.[46] He had producing properties in Kansas, Texas, and Oklahoma. He had acquired much wildcat acreage in these three states as well as in Arkansas, Louisiana, Mississippi, and New Mexico. But the climb back to the top had taken a toll on Tom Slick. Only in Texas and Kansas did he implement his plans to reduce his work load. He worked strenuously on his Oklahoma properties, despite his declining physical condition. In June, 1930, he admitted himself to Johns Hopkins Hospital in Baltimore, Maryland where he hoped he would regain his health.[47]

8

"My Whole Life Has Been Work, Work, Work"

There was only one Tom Slick. He is now gone by
the only route that could defeat him.

H. H. Champlin

During the summer of 1930, Slick had assembled one of the largest oil op-
erations in the Oklahoma City field with forty-five wells being drilled, more
than thirty wells completed, and almost 200,000 barrels of potential daily
production.[1] In addition, he had various interests under way in Kansas and
Texas. But Slick's frantic pace during the last several months of his life had
drained his health. On June 27, 1930, he admitted himself to Johns Hopkins
Hospital in Baltimore, Maryland, where he hoped to take a long and thorough "rest cure." Within three weeks he had recuperated somewhat; nevertheless, on July 15 he dictated his will.[2]

While in the hospital, physicians discovered that Slick had a goiter, or an
inflammation of the thyroid gland. On August 5 he underwent surgery to
correct this malady, and he seemed to improve rapidly after the operation.
Family members were quite hopeful when Slick regained his strength. He
began walking in the hallways of the hospital and even ventured outside.
The family planned a two-week vacation to Canada, which would immedi-

ately follow his scheduled release on August 15. However, on the evening before his release, Slick suffered a mild stroke that paralyzed the right side of his body. By morning his condition improved slightly, but on the afternoon of August 16, 1930, he suffered a massive stroke and cerebral hemorrhage and died.[3]

Later that day a special railroad car carried the family and Slick's body to Clarion. Friends traveled from Oklahoma, Kansas, Texas, and elsewhere to attend the funeral, which was held on Monday, August 18. Reverend P. A. Galbraith of the Methodist Episcopal Church in Clarion conducted the services in the home of the oilman's mother, Mary Slick.[4] That afternoon Slick's body was interred. Berenice Slick and the children returned to Oklahoma City shortly after the funeral.

From 2:30 P.M. until 3:30 P.M. on August 18, 1930, oil derricks throughout the Oklahoma City field stood silent. In Tulsa the Oklahoma Union Railway halted operations briefly.[5] Both events served as tributes from the employees, friends, and others who could not attend Slick's funeral. They commemorated the end of a colorful career that had spanned a quarter century from the early days of the Oklahoma oil industry in 1905 to the Oklahoma City boom of 1930.

The family received some comfort in the fact that Slick was so widely remembered. Many newspapers in the Mid-Continent region carried news of Slick's passing, as well as newspapers in New York City, Baltimore, Chicago, Houston, Los Angeles, and Kansas City. Most of the articles contained reminiscences by the oil page editor or letters from readers who knew Slick. One farmer expressed the sentiments of many in a letter in which he described a visit to a friend. The writer noted, "To my question as to how he was prospering he answered with a broad grin, 'Tom Slick paid my mortgage.'"[6] Another person made a similar observation by writing, "It was Tom Slick, the lucky wildcatter, who put this part of the country on the oil map when he drilled . . . southeast of Coyle and [leased] about every available acre that he could get, paying the farmers many thousands of dollars for the same. Farms that had been mortgaged for years with little hope of them ever being cleared to the owner were paid off with Slick's lease and royalty money and many had a comfortable balance left for new automobiles and other luxuries that otherwise would have been unthought of."[7]

Besides the newspaper accounts, others used various means to express their sympathy and respect. The First National Bank and Trust of Oklahoma City, the Oklahoma City Producers Association, and even the City of Guthrie passed resolutions in honor of Slick.[8] These resolutions praised his honesty, character, ability, and knowledge of the oil industry. Ernest E. Kirkpatrick, Slick's business partner, wrote two poems in memory of his close friend.[9]

But not all had warm praise for Slick. Several newspapers lamented the fact that he failed in what they considered to be his social obligation—giving a large portion of his fortune to charity.[10] These and other negative comments resulted from their lack of knowledge about Slick's generous, unpublicized gifts. But a far more serious matter emerged in the days after Slick's death as his vast estate became embroiled in a protracted legal and political battle over the true value of his property and his legal place of residency for tax purposes.

Slick wrote his last will and testament while hospitalized in Baltimore, about one month before his death. The will to dispose of his large estate was written in the same manner as he conducted his business deals—simply and concisely. He established three trustees to administer the estate: his wife, Berenice; his partner and friend, Charles F. Urschel; and his brother-in-law and attorney, Arthur A. Seeligson. He directed the trustees to honor all of his contracts for drilling wells and purchasing leases and to pay all of his debts. They would also be responsible for managing his producing properties until they could be sold. All stocks, bonds, and other intangible property would be sold and the income placed in trust.[11]

The will provided generously for Slick's family. Berenice was given authority to use the interest on the trust to maintain and support herself and the three children. Once business affairs were settled she would receive one-third of the trust. The remaining two-thirds would be held for the children who would obtain or be paid interest from their shares at various times in their lives. Tom Jr.[12] and Earl would be paid five thousand per year between their twenty-first and twenty-fifth birthdays. From ages twenty-five to thirty they would be paid all of the interest from their share. Then on their thirtieth, forty-fifth, and fifty-fifth birthdays they would receive one-third of the principal of their share. The arrangements for Betty were different, as her father sought to protect her from the avarice of unscrupulous men. From ages eighteen until twenty-five she would be paid five thousand yearly. Thereafter, she would receive the full interest from her share but would never inherit directly her portion.[13] His mother received a yearly payment of five thousand dollars. These transactions, however, were for the future. Of immediate concern to the trustees was the probate of Tom Slick's will.

Within two weeks of Slick's death, Oklahoma newspapers began gleefully proclaiming that the inheritance taxes on the huge Slick estate would be adequate to retire the state's debt and have enough money left to help during the hard times ahead. By this date the Great Depression had been deepening for nearly one year. Virtually every account placed the value of his estate at between $35,000,000 and $100,000,000. Taxes on the lower figure would have amounted to more than $4,000,000. One report stated that "such a tax payment would be a godsend to the stricken state treasury," which already had a deficit of $1,000,000.[14] But such estimates had little basis in fact. Oklahoma inheritance tax laws had three features pertinent to the Slick estate. First, they permitted taxation on tangible and intangible property of residents. Second, a resident's intangible property controlled by a foreign or out-of-state corporation could not be taxed. And third, for a nonresident, only their tangible Oklahoma property could be taxed.[15] Since Slick's vast holdings were vested in stocks of the Tom Slick Oil Company, a Delaware corporation, Oklahoma could not tax this property.

Under federal tax laws in 1930, the United States Internal Revenue Service assessed a graduated tax figure on each estate, depending on its total value. Of this tax, the IRS required payment of only 20 percent while the remaining 80 percent of the taxes could be credited to payment of state taxes. Most states had tax laws that claimed the decedent's tax would automatically be 80 percent of whatever figure the IRS declared.[16] Therefore, a great deal depended on whether Oklahoma could prove that Slick was one of its residents.

The trustees, however, hoped to establish Pennsylvania as the oilman's legal domicile because that state had lower tax rates on property.[17] To accomplish this the trustees filed a petition in Clarion to have the will probated under Pennsylvania laws. They also petitioned the Oklahoma County Court to probate the document as a foreign, or out-of-state, will. On September 29, 1930, Oklahoma County judge (Cicero) C. C. Christison decreed that the will would be accepted as foreign. At this point appraisers should have been appointed to fix the value of the estate. Then an equitable settlement would have been arranged. Instead, a lengthy and highly politicized court battle ensued over Slick's true domicile.

William H. Murray, one of Oklahoma's most colorful and controversial politicians, took to the stump in the fall of 1930 and was elected governor. In the course of his campaign he had garnered support by criticizing the current administration of William J. Holloway. The governor-elect charged Holloway and others with fiscal mismanagement and promised that he would pursue all tax-dodgers until they paid their fair share. Murray vowed to establish a special agency with the responsibility of collecting taxes. But with his aggressive tactics he had also alienated other incumbent and newly elected officials, among these Attorney General J. Berry King and Auditor-elect Frank C. Carter.

The situation exploded on January 6, 1931, when Murray filed a lawsuit in Oklahoma County Court accusing high state officials of making a secret and illegal deal to collect the Slick inheritance taxes. Named in the suit were outgoing auditor A. S. J. Shaw, Frank C. Carter, and the trustees of the Slick estate. Unnamed, but clearly implicated, were King and Holloway. Murray said he had good evidence that Shaw and Holloway had signed a contract that would empower Holloway to act as attorney in collecting the Slick taxes once he left office. The two men, Murray claimed, signed the contract with the written approval of King, and at least tacit agreement by Carter. Such a contract was legal under an Oklahoma law, which permitted the state auditor, "with the consent and approval of the Attorney General, to enter into a contract with any licensed attorney to collect inheritance tax from estates or property of *nonresident decedents*"[18] (emphasis added). However, Murray asserted that secret provisions of the contract allowed Holloway to collect an exorbitant fee of $500,000 for his services. In addition, Slick trustees and the Auditor (Shaw) had agreed to establish the value of the Slick estate at $10,000,000 rather than the amount Murray thought it was worth—approximately $50,000,000. Murray alleged that under the terms of this contract, "this plaintiff and the tax-payers of the State of Oklahoma would loose [*sic*] the approximate sum of $5,750,000.00 in inheritance taxes thereby defrauding the State of a large sum in taxes that rightfully and lawfully should be paid into the State Treasury for the use and benefit of the tax-payers of this State."[19] To prevent this alleged fraud, Murray asked the court to issue a restraining order to halt consummation of the contract.

The lawsuit stunned King and Holloway. King acted instantly to counter the charges that Murray made. On the same day the charges were filed, King composed a terse letter to Murray. King wrote that Murray's contention that he approved of the purported Holloway-Shaw contract was "preposterous and so utterly false." He stated that as early as September 1930 he believed that Slick should be considered a resident of Oklahoma, therefore making it unnecessary to contract for collection of the taxes. King pointed out that in September former governor J. B. A. Robertson tried to obtain a contract for this purpose, but King had refused to give his approval.[20] King further noted that he had no knowledge of a similar contract with Holloway and seriously doubted its existence. In closing, King took the opportunity to offer Murray some advice: "As an incoming Executive of Oklahoma you should be warned against lobby gossip and slaughterhouse scandal. Failure to resist both will subject any official to hazardous situations. This warning, of course, is gratuitous."[21]

Two days later, on January 8, Holloway took actions that seemed to verify his claim that he had not signed a contract with Shaw. Holloway stated that he had no knowledge of any negotiations to collect Slick's taxes. He instructed King by official letter to "institute whatever proceedings may be deemed necessary to the end that my original orders for the collection of this tax in the settlement of this estate may be met, and that if it is found that there is any truth in the allegations contained in [Murray's charges] which incriminate anybody, I want to here and now direct you to institute immediately criminal actions [for the] protection of the State and vindication of the State's interest."[22]

King acted promptly. He petitioned the Oklahoma County Court to allow him to intervene on behalf of the state and the defendants. He was certain that no laws had been broken. Instead, King focused on the fact that Murray had stated in his petition that Slick was a nonresident of Oklahoma. King feared that the governor-elect's statement in the court document would prejudice the state's attempt to prove that Slick was actually a resident. He wanted the Murray petition dismissed because it endangered the state's interests.[23] If Oklahoma could prove Slick's residency, then it would be entitled to a greater share of taxes.

As for the criminal allegations, King, Shaw, and Carter decided to force Murray's hand. On January 9 a county judge issued a subpoena requiring Murray to appear before the court and substantiate his charges. His appearance was set for Saturday, January 10. Timing seemed to be a critical factor because on January 12, Murray would be inaugurated as governor. As both sides appeared to be on course for a confrontation, Murray announced that he would disobey the subpoena. He planned instead to attend a class reunion in Norman, Oklahoma, that his former classmates were giving in his honor. Murray issued a simple statement in defense of his actions: "I have sent my excuses to the judge. I would rather go to jail for contempt of court than miss the reunion of my old schoolmates, some of whom I have not seen in 40 years."[24]

The defendants were outraged. Carter made perhaps the most irate denunciation of Murray's statement. He accused Murray of attempting to stall the proceedings until after he was sworn in as governor, saying, "I did not believe he ever intended to appear in Court . . . knowing that he would have Executive immunity and could not be compelled to attend after he takes the oath of office as Governor on Monday." Carter continued, "I now renew my demand for him to give not only to the Court, but the public, the full facts in this matter. His failure to appear Saturday or to make a statement to the public will be conclusive proof to any honest and intelligent person that his charge is frivolous, false and founded in venom and animosity."[25]

Others also began to suspect that Murray's charges may have had strictly political motivations. A columnist for an Oklahoma City newspaper observed that "men have some right to be secure in their good names, against suits based on gossip. Had Mr. Murray had grounds for suspicion, a warning of exposure unless they desisted, would have ended the conspiracy, had one existed. There was no need to take a chance of doing someone a wrong. Whether a mistaken idea of duty, an impulse to be spectacular, or a malicious desire to destroy someone, prompted Mr. Murray, we cannot say. We feel that he did a grave injustice to others. He did himself a graver injustice, if our conclusions prove to be right."[26] King seemed convinced from the beginning that Murray's primary motivation in bringing the charges was political. His goal was to discredit Governor Holloway and to embarrass King, Carter, and Shaw because they proved unwilling to fall under his political sway. Murray confirmed King's assumptions when he began threatening to reduce the attorney general's power and effectiveness. The governor-elect promised that when he took office he would reduce King's staff from eleven assistants to six.[27]

On the morning of January 10 the defendants gathered at the Oklahoma County Court to await the arrival of Murray or his lawyers. True to his word, Murray did not appear. Instead, his attorneys Claude Weaver and R. P. Hill entered the courtroom and stunned the defendants once again, this time by dismissing the charges. This meant that Murray could not be cited for contempt, but it also seemed to prove that King, Carter, Shaw, Holloway, and the Slick trustees had been correct in their assertions that Murray's actions were politically motivated. Hill, however, claimed that Murray had not conceded his charges and would in fact refile the case after his inauguration. But it seemed clear that Murray's bluff had been called, and he had lost. King told reporters that he hoped "the citizens of this state will profit by this example of hasty acceptance of street scandal whispered against public officials."[28] Carter noted simply, "There was no truth in the charge when filed. The voluntary dismissal is the best evidence that none exists now."[29] Murray never offered a detailed explanation of the dismissal, but he certainly must have realized that his statement calling Slick a nonresident could seriously jeopardize the state's attempt to prove his residency. Perhaps the best evidence of the frivolous and political nature of the lawsuit came from Murray himself several days later when he informed a newspaper reporter of a conversation he had with Slick estate lawyers on the day that he dismissed the charges. Murray noted, "I merely jollied with them and tried to impress them without saying so that I knew nothing."[30]

The new governor proved unwilling to allow his enemies (King and Carter) to gain any advantage in the political controversy. Murray set out immediately to take control of the tax collection process. After Murray took office, the first bill passed by the Oklahoma House of Representatives established the Oklahoma Tax Commission. The commission had among its many responsibilities the task of collecting inheritance taxes. Murray appointed a friend and supporter, Melven Cornish, as the first chairman of the tax commission. Cornish proceeded at once in the Slick tax matter. On March 6, 1931, he filed a motion in the county court, on behalf of the state, which sought to revoke the order Judge Christison issued that accepted the Slick will as foreign.[31] He hoped the state could compile enough evidence to prove that Slick could be declared a bona fide resident at the time of his death. Meanwhile, Pennsylvania attorneys for the Slick trustees gathered facts to prove his residency there.

Several key factors favored the claim of Oklahoma. Most important was the first provision of Slick's will in which he wrote, "I hereby give, devise and bequeath to my beloved wife, Berenice Slick, the homestead, which is the property where we now live, being located at the corner of Eighteenth Street and Hudson Street, in Oklahoma City, Oklahoma."[32] The state claimed that since 1926 Slick had owned this home located at 327 West Eighteenth Street. Officials further stated that the bulk of Slick's oil property was located within the state. Another key factor emerged when the Oklahoma County tax ferret furnished Cornish with an affidavit on which Slick had cited his residence as Oklahoma City. This document, attached to the charter for the Tom Slick Oil Company, was signed by Slick on April 18, 1929.[33]

W. N. Stokes of Oklahoma City and Harry S. Rugh of Clarion, attorneys for the Slick trustees, found a great deal of contrary evidence, however, which tended to favor the claim of Pennsylvania. They discovered that the title for Slick's home in Oklahoma City was in Berenice's name. They also noted that the bulk of Slick's Oklahoma oil holdings were vested in shares of Tom Slick Oil, a Delaware corporation. This meant that Oklahoma would be ineligible to collect taxes if Slick could be proven to be a resident of Pennsylvania. The attorneys uncovered other points as well. They discovered that from 1911 to 1930 Slick maintained his voter registration in Clarion. The title to his home in Clarion was in his name. In addition, they found many witnesses willing to testify that Slick always intended to maintain his residence in Clarion.[34]

Two lawsuits involving Slick shortly before his death further enhanced the contentions of the trustees. In the first suit, *W. A. Field v. T. B. Slick*, December 1929, Slick provided testimony concerning his residency. He confirmed that he had owned his home in Clarion since 1915 and considered it to be his residence. Slick responded to other questions from his attorney:

Q. In the conduct of your business, in the writing of contracts in which it is neces-sary to state your residence, I will ask you where that is always recited as being?

A. Clarion, Pennsylvania.

Q. In rendering your personal income tax returns, are they rendered as from Clarion or Oklahoma City?

A. Well, the other boys handle that, but I imagine always from Clarion, Pennsyl-vania.

Q. Have you ever elected or declared your intention of abandoning your resi-dence and citizenship in Pennsylvania for that in Oklahoma?

A. No, sir.[35]

In another case filed in February 1930, *William Hassell v. T. B. Slick, et al.,* the defendants claimed that the suit should be dismissed from the Oklahoma County Court because it had no jurisdiction. They based this claim on the fact that all of the defendants were nonresidents of Oklahoma. The court agreed and issued an order for dismissal.[36]

The Oklahoma Supreme Court reached a decision in December 1930 that had an important impact on the issue of Slick's residency. In *Richards v. Huff,* the state's highest court ruled that domicile "may be regarded, in our com-monlaw sense, as the place where one has his true, fixed, and permanent home and principal establishment, and to which, whenever he is absent, he has the intention of returning." The justices further decided that "to effect a change of residence or domicile, there must be an actual abandonment of the first domi-cile, coupled with an intention not to return to it, and there must be a new domicile acquired by actual residence in another place . . . with the intention of making the last acquired residence a permanent home."[37] Stokes and Rugh realized the importance of this decision in their efforts on behalf of the Slick trustees and discussed the merits of the case in their correspondence.[38] The two attorneys likewise believed that Oklahoma was bound to accept Judge Christison's order that admitted Slick's will to probate as a foreign will.

On the political and legal battleground Murray and the state legislature worked quickly to maximize the tax revenues that Oklahoma might obtain. Murray received word from W. T. McConnell, an attorney associated with the auditor's office in the Holloway administration, that the current Okla-homa inheritance tax law (of 1927) could possibly be challenged by the Slick trustees. McConnell informed Murray that the state senate had passed this law in violation of procedural rules and thus it might be challenged by the Slick trustees as unconstitutional. He urged Murray to have the law quickly reenacted and even amended to set a higher tax rate because the tax payment due would be "enough to wipe out the present deficit."[39] On March 23, 1931, only three days after McConnell wrote to Murray, legislators introduced a bill to amend and essentially reenact the 1927 inheritance tax law! This bill became law on April 4, 1931.[40] The *Daily Oklahoman* correctly observed that the new law had been passed "to facilitate the collection of taxes from the Slick estate."[41]

Meanwhile, the tax commission seemed to reach an impasse in its efforts to prove Slick's residency. To break the deadlock, the trustees for the Slick estate proposed to the tax commission that perhaps some sort of compromise settlement might be reached. Ironically, the commissioners decided to seek the advice of Attorney General King on the matter of the proposed compromise.[42] King used this pretext to respond with the type of invective that Murray and his supporters could inspire in their enemies. In a letter to the tax commission, King recounted the events leading to Murray's lawsuit in January 1931, then offered other observations about the governor's handling of the Slick tax matter:

I entertain respect for you as individuals, but it is needless for me to tell you that I am cognizant of the fact that you are entirely subservient to the will and wish of the Chief Executive of this State, who has so conducted himself personally as to forfeit my personal respect. . . . Citizen Murray [in January 1931] had not been back from Bolivia sufficiently long to have satisfied his innate ego for front page publicity, and to be consistent with his never ceasing struggle to satisfy personal vanity, he sought this as a means of arrogating unto himself further publicity through the slanderous suggestion of irresponsible busy-bodies who then sought, and continue to seek, patronage from his gullible gubernatorial hand. He forsaw [*sic*] an opportunity to ride on the crest of publicity's wave, hoping at the same time to submerge the outgoing Governor and to discredit the incoming Auditor as well as myself, whom he had found he could not dominate with the same degree of intolerable control that he has exercised over most of his sycophants in appointee capacity and other fawning and intimidated employees and officials who hope to hold their positions and pay-checks under his administration. I have no desire to wreck the administrative program of Governor Murray. I am quite content to permit him through his own indiscretion, inconsistency and utter ignorance to wreck himself. . . . It would be humorous, if not so serious, for me now to point out that you, as Mr. Murray boastfully denominates you "His Commission," should now appeal to me to assist you in a duty that he has arrogantly announced I was disqualified and unfit to perform in January.[43]

In addition to such vituperation in correspondence, King hounded Murray and the tax commission in the press to explain why the Slick taxes remained uncollected one year after Murray had taken office.[44] Murray would not answer.

Despite the mudslinging, the proposal for a compromise settlement of the taxes received serious consideration and eventually served as the basis for adjustment of differences between Oklahoma and Pennsylvania. The trustees suggested that the value of the estate would amount to about $10,000,000. Oklahoma officials claimed this estimate was far too low and guessed the value should range between $35,000,000 and $100,000,000. Finally, more than two years after Slick's death, the court appointed four consultants to appraise the true value of the oilman's estate. This difficult task was assigned to J. J. Monroney, John A. Silsbee, Leonard H. Logan, and H. E. Musson in September 1932.[45]

Within two months the appraisers learned how far-flung the interests and holdings of Tom Slick had been. The valuation filled four volumes, a total of more than 1,100 pages of text, maps, and charts. They found that Slick owned almost $5,000,000 worth of oil properties. He owned a fleet of twenty-nine trucks and automobiles. Slick held more than $3,000,000 worth of stock, mostly in other oil companies like Prairie, Gulf, Sinclair, Royal Dutch, and Standard of New Jersey. He invested more than $10,000,000 in bonds for schools, highways, water districts, as well as municipal and United States bonds. Along with cash and other income, the appraisers placed the value of Slick's assets at $23,232,179.62. On the debit side, Slick owed more than $16,000,000 in debts, taxes, and fees. This placed the net value of the estate, as of August 15, 1930, at $6,712,960.02.[46]

Oklahoma officials could barely accept the fact that the appraisal was so low. Nevertheless, they consented to begin negotiations with Stokes to reach an agreement that would settle the tax issue promptly and avoid a risky court battle. Oklahoma felt additional pressure to negotiate a settlement because the IRS had certified the estate appraisal and taxed it accordingly.[47] Kansas, Texas, and Mississippi, states that also had tax claims against the estate, accepted the appraisal.

After more than two years, the estate, Pennsylvania, and Oklahoma agreed to terms that gave the dispute an ironic conclusion. Stokes made his proposal in a confidential letter to Robert M. Rainey, an Oklahoma City attorney representing Pennsylvania's interests. Stokes offered that if Oklahoma would dismiss its actions against the Slick estate—that is, admit that Slick was a nonresident—the trustees would pay taxes as though Slick had been a resident![48] Pennsylvania officials had to choose whether to accept a compromise sum or wage an expensive court battle to obtain a larger share. Rainey sent a telegram to the Pennsylvania attorney general to inquire if they would agree to Stokes's proposal:

> The executors of the Slick estate are trying to make settlement with Oklahoma and as a basis therefor desire an expression from the Pennsylvania authorities as to whether Pennsylvania will accept the difference between the amount of taxes agreed upon by the Slick estate with Oklahoma and the amount paid Kansas, Mississippi and Texas, provided this difference to be paid Pennsylvania will amount to at least three hundred fifty thousand dollars. If this is agreeable please authorize me to so advise the executors of the estate.[49]

The Pennsylvania attorney general responded immediately and accepted the proposal as a basis for settlement.[50]

On November 12, 1932, Stokes and a representative for the Oklahoma Tax Commission appeared before Judge Christison for the final hearing on the Slick tax matter. According to terms of the agreement, the IRS assessed taxes at a figure of $970,227.15, of which the federal treasury retained 20 percent, or $194,045.43. The attorneys divided the remaining 80 percent among the interested states: Oklahoma, $414,183.43; Pennsylvania, $353,135.43; Kansas, $6,344.83; Texas, $1,521.16; and Mississippi, $996.87.[51]

Thus ended the protracted dispute. Oklahoma clearly did not obtain enough to retire its debt as so many had hoped. By late 1932 Murray and other state officials had lost interest in the Slick tax case, especially after it became apparent that the estate was smaller than expected and that any attempt to recover a larger portion of the taxes would involve a costly court battle. Besides, Murray's antics with the Oklahoma National Guard, the intense oil crisis, and the deepening grip of the Great Depression commanded the public's attention to a greater degree. The delay in settling the estate had also complicated the management of Slick's properties. Virtually every important business decision required court approval while the case was pending. Overall, the prolonged dispute seemed a rather demeaning conclusion for the exciting and colorful career of Tom Slick.

Slick's death at the relatively young age of forty-six cut short a twenty-year career that spanned the emergence and early dominance of the Mid-Continent field. The development of oil permanently altered the economies of Oklahoma, Kansas, and Texas. In a national context, Mid-Continent oil helped meet the growing demand for petroleum in the industrial, commercial, and private sectors of the American economy. It was largely independents like Tom Slick who searched for and produced the oil that met this rising demand.

In the process, Slick had become one of the largest independents and had earned several fortunes in an industry that had changed significantly since his early days at Cushing. In 1912 oilmen sought to find and produce the oil as quickly as possible before competitors arrived on the scene and before the price of oil dropped. Demand seemed unlimited. With little capital and a portable drilling rig almost anyone could take a chance. By 1930, with the flush production at Seminole, Oklahoma City, and the emerging East Texas fields, prices dropped precipitously. Higher drilling costs and the onset of the Great Depression also discouraged new entrants into the oil business. In 1930 the industry stood on the verge of coming under full government regulation.

Throughout the course of his career Tom Slick embodied many of the general characteristics of independent oilmen of his day, and in several positive ways his aggressive business tendencies fit in well with the business environment of the 1920s. He had, perhaps to an excessive degree, that gambler, risk-taker spirit that led him to speculate on oil prospects all through the Mid-Continent field. Slick emerged as one of the clear leaders in finding and developing oil pools. He broadened his chances at success by spreading his risks geographically, even though he occasionally sought to spread his financial risks by branching out into other business ventures. Nevertheless, he always came back to the same aspects of the industry—exploration and production.[52] Slick also enhanced his chances of success, like other independents, through his growing acceptance of geology as a tool for finding oil. As the industry changed and moved toward government regulation, Slick stood ready to make some changes as well. He implemented various conservation measures such as well spacing and unitization. He welcomed limited governmental control as a means of rationalizing the industry, but Slick primarily stressed self-regulation as the best means of accomplishing this purpose.

While he shared many of the same patterns of business behavior as other independents, Slick differed in some important ways. After his initial success, records failed to reveal any reliance upon outside capital to fund his drilling ventures. In fact, Slick and others commented upon this circumstance, noting that he was one of the few independents who had enough money to drill a well "straight up," or, on his own.[53] This left him in thorough control of his own operations.

Slick's chronic health problems also impacted the ways in which he conducted his operations. He worked at a frenetic pace until he built up substantial holdings; then he would cite poor health as his primary reason for selling his operations. Whether Slick sold his holdings purely for reasons of declining health or merely to raise capital for his next foray, a common tactic for many independents, cannot be positively determined. It was likely that in Slick's case these purposes coincided, but, on the surface at least, Slick's career appeared to be a constant struggle between staying in "the game" and being forced out by illness.

Yet another difference was Slick's immediate interest and leadership role in the growing conservation movement of the late 1920s. He emerged as an outspoken opponent of proration as harmful to independents and offered counterproposals such as the Sunday shutdown agreement. He commanded the respect of independents, and many looked to him as a spokesman for their general interests. He also embraced the techniques of unitization and well spacing as the best means of raising oil prices and conservatively producing a pool of oil. Slick, normally reticent and extraordinarily private, so vigorously supported these strategies that he behaved in uncharacteristic ways—giving speeches, making statements published by the press, and sponsoring a social event for oilmen to discuss conservation issues.

Slick's almost pathological aversion to publicity was a hallmark of his character. He steadfastly refused to make his business or personal life public knowledge. The irony was, of course, that he could not avoid being a public figure. Anyone who enjoyed his level of success in an industry as publicized and romanticized as oil would attract public attention. In fact, at the time of his death, public media noted that Slick had amassed leases in virtually every prospective oil and gas area of the Mid-Continent region. Had he lived it is entirely reasonable to assume that his tremendous success would have continued and that he would have remained in the public eye.

Tom Slick had a colorful career in the Oklahoma, Kansas, and Texas oil industry. Virtually every source that mentions his name recounts his famous leasing stunt at Cushing. Even a 1990 production from Oklahoma's public television system entitled "Oklahoma Passage," a miniseries saga of the state's history, briefly described the Cushing episode. But his notoriety rested equally on his phenomenal success. Many newspapers in the 1920s carried stories that followed his activities and discoveries throughout the Mid-Continent. Most sources contained anecdotes that attested to his uncanny good luck in finding oil and his honesty.[54] This remarkable measure of success made Tom Slick somewhat of a legend as one of those independent oilmen who explored and developed the numerous pools that made the Mid-Continent one of the greatest oil fields ever discovered.

Epilogue

Business associates of Slick continue his policy—
'work.' Drilling is going ahead daily in the 38 Slick
wells here, all located in proven areas. While Slick
will not be in the 'dog house' or sitting on the 'lazy
bench' to watch his latest gusher spatter the sur-
rounding landscape with oil and gas, as he loved
to do in his lifetime, his associates know that it
was among his last wishes that they 'carry on.'

Oklahoma City News

With the theme "Hats Off to Wildcatters," the annual Renaissance Ball at
the Marland Mansion in Ponca City, Oklahoma, served as the backdrop for
the 1988 posthumous induction of Tom Slick into the National Petroleum
Hall of Fame. His portrait took its place in a gallery of the Marland Mansion with past inductees E. W. Marland, Frank Phillips, Earle Haliburton,
Lew Wentz, Robert S. Kerr, William Skelly, and Harry Sinclair, among many
others. The award was granted in recognition of a career that had ended
almost fifty-eight years before.

Shortly after Slick's untimely death, Urschel began working to consolidate and incorporate the various interests and properties owned by the oilman. Urschel grouped most of Slick's holdings under two new corporations,

Tom Slick Properties, Inc., and Slick-Urschel Oil Company. Kirkpatrick continued his employment by assisting Urschel in managing the Slick estate. Most of the operations under way at the time of Slick's death continued until 1937. In that year, however, Urschel dissolved Slick, Pryor, and Lockhart and sold most of what had been Slick's oil properties to the Transwestern Oil Company.[1]

The Slick family also experienced important changes in the years after the oilman's death. In April of 1931, Flored Slick, Tom's sister and wife of Charles Urschel, died. She too passed away at a relatively young age, only thirty-eight. Late in 1932 the two families joined again when Charles Urschel married Berenice Slick. Urschel already served as a legal guardian of the Slick children and now became their stepfather. His positive influence came at an important time in their lives as all three children entered their adolescent years.

In 1933 one of the most sensational crimes of the gangster era occurred in Oklahoma City. Shortly before his death, Slick became aware of a rumor that he might be the target of a gang-related kidnapping. Slick and his wife even feared that one of their children might be the victim. This came in the wake of the news stories on Slick's huge sellout to Prairie Oil and Gas. But Slick died before such a crime took place. Late in the evening on July 22, 1933, George "Machine Gun" Kelly and Albert Bates intruded on a late-night bridge game at the Urschel residence and kidnapped Charles Urschel. After the family paid his ransom, Urschel helped the Federal Bureau of Investigation solve the case. He provided the FBI with numerous details about his captors, the hideout where they held him, the directions they traveled, and the weather. Most important, he noted the daily passage of an airplane during his nine-day captivity. With these clues, the FBI found the farmhouse near Paradise, Texas, where Kelly and Bates had held Urschel captive. The outlaws were finally caught, tried, and sentenced to life in prison.[2]

As for the Slick children, it was only natural that they should become interested in oil. As Tom Jr. once remarked, "Two sons and a daughter could not be raised as close to the oil industry as we were, without being inoculated with at least a light case of the virus of excitement and romance of that industry."[3] The trio, along with Urschel and Charles Urschel, Jr., operated in various combinations of partnership. They drilled with success principally in south and west Texas, but also in Mississippi. In February 1942, they discovered the South Caesar Field in Bee County, Texas. The following year they opened the Slick-Wilcox Field, which straddled the boundary between DeWitt and Goliad Counties in Texas. The discoveries continued in 1947 when they found the Ruhman Field, also in Bee County.[4]

The greatest discovery came in 1948 when headlines proclaimed that "Tom Slick, Jr. Succeeds to Throne of 'King of Wildcatters.'"[5] The year before, Tom Jr. had taken over a well from the famous wildcatter Mike Benedum. Benedum had begun the well in 1941 on a large block of acreage in Upton County, just southeast of Odessa, Texas. Drilling halted at 10,000 feet, however, after the crew encountered numerous problems and had not found oil. After receiving interest in a large percentage of the acreage around the well as part of the deal, Slick took over the drilling. He used the latest techniques and equipment in bringing the well to completion. It proved to be the discovery well of the Benedum Field when drillers found a tremendous oil sand at a depth of over 12,000 feet.[6]

Despite these successes, oil was not the central focus of the Slick children. Tom Jr. had perhaps the broadest range of interests. A graduate of Yale University and former student at Harvard University and the Massachusetts Institute of Technology, Tom Jr. had ideas and enough money to back them. With a deep interest in science, he founded the Southwest Foundation for Research and Education in 1941; the Southwest Research Institute, 1947; and the Institute for Inventive Research, 1948. These institutions conducted research in medicine, agriculture, and animal husbandry and encouraged the development of inventions for a wide variety of applications. He based all of these in his adopted hometown of San Antonio, Texas. In addition, Tom Jr. wrote two books on world peace, invented the lift-slab method in construction of buildings, and searched the Himalayas of Nepal for the yeti.[7] Earl Slick found his career in aviation. He served as a pilot in the Air Transport Command during World War II. After the war he bought nine surplus cargo planes from the United States government and used them to carry produce, frozen foods, heavy equipment, and other commercial cargo. Within five years his Slick Airways became the largest air transport business in the country.[8] Betty and her husband were partners in Slick-Moorman Oil, which achieved success in Texas oil. She later founded the Argyle Club of San Antonio. This private club dedicates a portion of its income to assist in funding the Southwest Research Institute. She also became quite active in various civic groups in San Antonio.[9]

All three of Slick's children have made important contributions in their chosen areas of work and in their communities. Their drive, their spirit of adventure, and their willingness to take risks in their various business interests all may be seen as part of their father's legacy. Clearly, Tom Slick had left his imprint upon them and upon the industry in which he became the "King of the Wildcatters."

Notes

Introduction. "I Don't Like Publicity"

1. *Daily Oklahoman,* March 31, 1929.
2. Knowles, *Greatest Gamblers,* 11–12.
3. Getty, *My Life and Fortunes,* 57.
4. *Tulsa Daily World,* February 12, 1927.
5. *Kansas City Star,* May 5, 1929.
6. Clifford L. Frates, interview by author, Oklahoma City, Okla., August 8, 1986. Frates was Tom Slick's brother-in-law.
7. Forbes, "Passing of the Small Oil Man"; Williamson, et al., *American Petroleum Industry,* 34–35; Rister, *Oil!,* 128.
8. Olien and Olien, *Wildcatters,* 8–9.
9. Owen, *Trek of the Oil Finders,* 292–94.
10. Ross, *Preliminary Report,* 11.
11. Merlin Cook, interview by author, San Antonio, Tex., August 8, 1986. Cook worked as a production accountant for Slick.
12. These oil-related terms are defined in the glossary.
13. Mathews, *Life and Death of an Oilman,* 151–52.
14. Hurt, *Texas Rich,* 57.
15. On several occasions Slick went against the advice of geological consultants and drilled on acreage condemned by them, most notably at Pioneer, Texas; Tonkawa; and Seminole. All three of these locations produced tremendous quantities of oil. In another case of daring drilling, he drilled on the nonproductive side of a geological fault line in the Oklahoma City field. Only one geologist, Billy Atkinson, agreed with Slick that oil might be found across the fault line. When the well came in as a large

producer, Slick hired Atkinson as his geologist. (See the Merlin Cook interview, August 8, 1986.)

16. *Daily Oklahoman,* March 31, 1929.

17. Arthur A. Seeligson, Jr. interview by author, San Antonio, Tex., July 29, 1986.

18. Martha Rugh Platt, interview by author, Minneapolis, Minn., October 21, 1989. Platt is the daughter of Harry Rugh, an attorney who handled some legal matters for Slick. She told of one such fishing trip that her family and the Slicks took to Ontario, Canada, in 1925.

19. Ibid.

20. *Daily Oklahoman,* March 31, 1929.

21. *Kansas City Star,* May 5, 1929.

22. "Resolution on the Death of Thomas B. Slick," by Board of Directors, First National Bank and Trust Company, Oklahoma City, Okla., n.d. This document was part of Betty Moorman's scrapbook. As a note of interest, Slick had served as a member of the board of directors, along with his friend B. B. Jones, since October 1927.

23. Martha Rugh Platt, letter to author, May 13, 1986.

24. T. B. Slick, letter to Mr. and Mrs. Harry E. Rugh, January 19, 1925, in possession of the author.

25. *Kansas City Star,* May 5, 1929.

26. Ibid.

27. Ibid.

28. Platt letter, May 13, 1986; *Kansas City Star,* May 5, 1929; *Daily Oklahoman,* March 31, 1929; Betty Slick Moorman, interview by author, San Antonio, Tex., July 28, 1986. Moorman is Tom Slick's daughter. She remembered her father would take them fishing and for walks. He took them to visit his oil wells, taught them to play bridge, and interacted with his children as would any normal father. However, he was always quite busy, and she categorized him as a "workaholic."

29. *Kansas City Star,* May 5, 1929.

30. Jack T. Conn, letter to Kenny Franks, Oklahoma Heritage Association, Oklahoma City, September 25, 1978. Conn, a well-known Oklahoma oilman and a contemporary of Slick, wrote this letter recounting stories told to him by Charles Urschel, Jr., Slick's nephew, while they were on a private fishing trip in Canada.

31. Williamson, et al., *Age of Energy,* 3–4, 15–29.

Chapter 1. "I'm a Born Trader"

1. *Kansas City Star,* May 5, 1929.

2. *Clarion Democrat,* July 18, 1901; Charles U. Slick, interview by author, Atlanta, Ga., October 19, 1989. Charles Slick is the grandson of Tom Slick. In 1983 he hired a professional genealogist to research his family's background. Much of the genealogical information contained in this chapter has been furnished by him.

3. Katrina Baker Showers, letter to Charles F. Urschel, Jr., December 12, 1978, in possession of Charles U. Slick. Showers was one of Tom Slick's distant cousins.

4. Charles U. Slick interview, October 19, 1989.

5. Ibid.

6. *Clarion Democrat,* September 29, 1892; October 13, 1892.

7. Ibid., August 21, 1930. Tom Slick, Jr., for some reason, provided an account of his father's early life that had so many factual errors that all of the story must be discounted. He made the following remarks in 1952 at an "Old Timers' Dinner" in Cushing, Oklahoma, where various oilmen gathered to commemorate the fortieth anniversary of the discovery of the Cushing field. As Slick, Jr., told the story:

> My father started life as a poor boy back in 1883 in Clarion, Pennsylvania, right in the region where the oil industry was born. His father before him had some connection with the early days of the oil industry as a drilling contractor, but he died in South America when my father was but eleven years old, leaving him as the oldest of three children, and a widowed wife who knew nothing of earning a living.
>
> My father left school and was able from that age on to support his family by such devices as selling newspapers and stove polish, buying chickens wholesale from the farmers, dressing them and then selling them retail to the customers.
>
> By the time he was eighteen, he went to work as a "roustabout" in the oil fields in West Virginia, and by the time he was twenty, he moved out to the very early days of the oil industry in Oklahoma—having been promoted, by that time, to cable tool dresser. (Thomas B. Slick, Jr., "Some Comments on . . . The Life of Tom Slick, Sr." n.p., September 9, 1952)

8. Baxter, "Thomas B. Slick," 2. Baxter, a friend and former employee of Slick, wrote a four-page memorial to Slick in the Prairie Oil and Gas Company's annual report. Baxter, as well as other sources, stated that Slick attended the State Normal School at Clarion. However, school records there, according to the archivist in charge of them, indicate that Slick never attended. Gerard B. McCabe, letter to author, November 1, 1989; McCabe is the director of libraries for Clarion University, the current name of that institution.

9. Charles U. Slick interview, October 19, 1989.

10. *Clarion Democrat,* September 29, 1892; August 3, 1894.

11. *Clarion Democrat,* June 14, 1894; July 26, 1894; October 26, 1899.

12. Much of the history of oil development in the area around Clarion, Pennsylvania, can be found in Carll, *Geology of the Oil Regions* and *Seventh Report on the Oil and Gas Fields,* and Ashley and Robinson, *Oil and Gas Fields of Pennsylvania.*

13. *Clarion Democrat,* July 9, 1896, notes the resurgence of the oil boom in Clarion; the *Clarion Democrat* from July to December 1896 notes the increasing activity.

14. *Chanute Daily Times,* June 5, 1903.

15. Wheaton, *Kansas-Indian Territory,* 91.

16. Ibid., 89.

17. Ibid., 90.

18. *Chanute Daily Tribune,* June 5, 1903. Many Pennsylvania and West Virginia

men made the trek along an arc through Indiana and Illinois to Kansas, Oklahoma, Texas, and Louisiana; some even continued on into Mexico and South America, while others veered toward Canada or California.

19. *Kansas City Star,* May 5, 1929; *Peru Oil Gazette,* June 1, 1904; *Peru Weekly Derrick,* June 4, 1904.

20. *Kansas City Star,* September 7, 1930.

21. *Clarion Democrat,* August 21, 1930.

22. *Kansas City Star,* May 5, 1929.

23. Ibid., September 7, 1930.

24. Ibid. Massey's comment about mushrooms referred to the fact that young Slick had a passion for these and other delicacies, such as rye bread, limburger cheese, and beer.

25. Ibid. Slick made a similar deal years later when he returned to Oklahoma to secure leases for Charles B. Shaffer. This gave him interest in some of the most productive leases in the Cushing field.

26. Ball, *This Fascinating Oil Business,* 85–97.

27. *Tryon News,* August 26, September 9, 1904.

28. Ibid., October 7, November 18, 25, December 2, 16, 1904.

29. Ibid., October 7, November 25, 1904.

30. *W. A. Field v. Thomas B. Slick,* case No. 61,575, Oklahoma County Court, 1929. "Deposition of T.B. Slick," January 15, 1930.

31. *Tryon News,* November 25, 1904.

32. Ibid.

33. Ibid., December 2, 16, 1904.

34. Ibid., January 6, 20, February 10, 1905. Slick did not use his father as the driller because he was probably still working for Massey in Kansas. However, his father visited him in Tryon at least twice. (*Tryon News,* January 6, 27, 1905.)

35. *Kansas City Star,* September 7, 1930; *Tryon News,* February 10, 17, March 31, 1905.

36. *Kansas City Star,* September 7, 1930.

37. *Yale Record,* March 16 and August 13, 1905.

38. *Perkins Journal,* June 16, 1905. In August 1905 Benedum and Trees discovered oil near Robinson, Illinois, which helped launch their fabulous career together. (See Mallison, *Great Wildcatter,* 149–74; and Knowles, *Greatest Gamblers,* 74–77.) Ironically, this new oil boom in Illinois attracted Slick there after his failures at Tryon and Kendrick.

39. *Perkins Journal,* May 19, 1905.

40. *Tryon News,* March 24, 1905.

41. Ibid., July 20, 1905.

42. Ibid., September 28, 1905. New businesses included a hotel and a lumber yard.

43. Ibid., March 3, 1905.

44. Ibid., June 22, 1905; *Kansas City Star,* September 7, 1930. Unfortunately, news on the Tryon well was impossible to ascertain after 1905. All files of the Tryon

paper for the year 1906 were missing. I checked the newspapers from Tulsa, Stillwater, Agra, Perkins, Kendrick, Cushing, Stroud, and Chandler but found no information. However, the drilling must have ended in early 1906. First of all, drilling commenced January 18, 1905, and by June 22, 1905, had only reached a depth of 1,600 feet. It is reasonable to assume that six months or more were required to reach 2,800 feet, since drilling usually became more difficult at greater depths. In addition, in January 1930 Tom Slick said that he worked in the Tryon area for a year and a half. This would mean that he left early in 1906. (See *W. A. Field v. Thomas B. Slick.*) Also, Massey took an extended vacation in the winter of 1905 and probably did not order Slick to cease drilling until he returned. (See *Kansas City Star,* September 7, 1930.) Massey likely insisted on stopping the well because this was much deeper than the wells he had drilled in Chautauqua County, Kansas. According to Craig Miner in *Discovery!* much of the oil discovered in this area of Kansas was found at depths of only 700–900 feet (89).

45. *Kansas City Star,* September 7, 1930. Massey might have spent as much as ten thousand dollars on this venture. This would have included leasing costs, outfitting Slick, building the office, and all of the expenses involved in drilling the well.

46. *W. A. Field v. Thomas B. Slick; Kendrick Dispatch,* August 10, 1906.

47. *Clarion Democrat,* October 26, November 9, 1905.

48. Ibid., November 9, 1905.

49. *Kansas City Star,* May 5, 1929.

Chapter 2. "Every Time I Drill a Well I Have to Get Another Partner"

The title of this chapter is a quip attributed to Tom Slick. During his numerous attempts to find oil in Creek County and other locales he had several financial backers for the various wells. See Craighead, "Cushing-Drumright Oil Rush," 25.

1. Drumright Historical Society; for precise location see Clarel B. Mapes, letter to Robert H. Dott, July 7, 1944, in Oklahoma Historical Data—Cushing Field file at the Mid-Continent Oil and Gas Association, Tulsa, Okla.

2. Newsom, *Drumright!,* 10; For more biographical information on Charles B. Shaffer see *Cushing Independent,* November 7, 1913. Shaffer moved westward from the oil fields of New York to Pennsylvania, West Virginia, Kentucky, Indiana, Illinois, and eventually to Kansas, Oklahoma, and Texas. Many years before, he had formed a partnership with E. E. Smathers, but in 1911 they established their offices in Chicago, where Slick went to request the loan to drill the Wheeler well. *W. A. Field v. Thomas B. Slick,* case No. 61,575, Oklahoma County Court, 1929, "Deposition of T. B. Slick," January 15, 1930. Finding this deposition was for me one of the thrills of researching. This lawsuit involved a simple traffic accident in which Field sued for damages. His lawyer questioned Slick at length about how he came to be in Oklahoma, his early years here, where he went when he left, where he lived during these years, etc. Normally, this deposition would *not* have been transcribed from the clerk's shorthand notes and thus the information contained in it would have been unavailable to me. When Slick died, however, the state of Oklahoma hoped to prove that he was a resident. Someone made the attorney general aware of Slick's remarks

at this trial, held only eight months before he died. Therefore, state officials had his testimony transcribed so it could be used as evidence against the Slick estate which claimed Pennsylvania as his state of residency.

3. *Cushing Daily Citizen,* March 19, 1952.

4. *Daily Oklahoman,* October 27, 1916.

5. Creek County Court records. This first lease was on the Will R. Dunlap farm just east of Bristow. Court lease records began with statehood in November, but Slick had leases in Creek County prior to this date.

6. Mrs. E. F. Kelley interview, Doris Duke Indian Oral History, vol. 44, T-180-2, Western History Collections, Norman, Okla., p. 6.

7. Tom Slick, Jr., interview, July 30, 1951. Benedum and the Oil Industry Collection, Oral History Collection, Columbia University, New York, N.Y., pp. 2–3.

8. Ibid. Dry holes drilled with Shaffer, Jones, unknown others, and by Slick alone were probably included in these ten wells.

9. *Bristow Record,* January 25, March 15, June 21, 1907.

10. Ibid., January 29, 1909; *Big Sandy News,* October 8, 1909.

11. *Bristow Record,* March 3, 10, and April 28, 1911; Slick and Jones bought out the others and kept this land for several years. It proved to be a great stroke of luck. See chapter 5, which deals with the Jennings pool in 1919–1920.

12. Ibid., August 4, 1911.

13. Newsom, *Drumright!,* 17.

14. Thoburn and Wright, *Oklahoma,* 3:400–401.

15. As a note of interest, the company was chartered on March 6, 1912, only eleven days before the Wheeler strike.

16. *Tulsa Daily World,* October 5, 1911. For precise well location, see Wood, "Oil and Gas Development," 37. This location was only two miles north of Drumright, which did not exist at that time.

17. *Tulsa Daily World,* November 14, 1911.

18. Ibid., November 15, 16, 1911.

19. Ibid., November 19, 1911.

20. Wood, "Oil and Gas Development," 37; *Tulsa Daily World,* October 22, 1914.

21. *Tulsa Daily World,* October 22, 1914. This well provides an example of the role that luck plays in the oil industry. Three years after Slick abandoned the well Shaffer returned and drilled deeper, bringing in a 10,000-barrel-per-day producer! A few weeks later Shaffer went a few feet deeper in hopes of raising output even higher but instead drilled through the oil sand. The hole then flooded with salt water, killing the well for weeks. The well eventually began producing again but only at an average level.

22. *Tulsa Daily World,* November 28, 1911.

23. *Cushing Democrat,* January 4, 1912; *Cushing Independent,* January 4, 1912; *Daily Oklahoman,* April 19, 1925; Newsom, *Drumright!,* 18.

24. Wood, "Oil and Gas Development," 37–38. The first well location section 2-T17N-R5E, second well location at section 4-T17N-R5E.

25. F. S. Barde Collection, "Oilfields—Cushing and Drumright," Box 9. Oklahoma Historical Society, Oklahoma City, Okla.

26. *Bristow Record*, June 5, 1913.

27. Newsom, *Drumright!*

28. Knowles, *Greatest Gamblers*, 196.

29. *Daily Oklahoman*, April 19, 1925; Newsom, *Drumright!*, 18; *Cushing Independent*, January 25, 1912.

30. They also selected a site on the Albert E. Barney farm in NW section 34-T18N-R7E. This well came in a few days after the Wheeler well as a five-million-cubic-feet gasser.

31. For the most exaggerated form of this story, see "Magic Knock of Fortune."

32. Newsom, *Drumright!*, 17.

33. *Cushing Independent*, January 25, 1912.

34. *Cushing Democrat*, February 1, 1912.

35. This incident and all of the information about the Gruvers came from telephone interviews with May and Clark Gruver (two of Jesse Gruver's children) by the author. It seems that the Gruvers knew the Slicks from their earlier days when they lived in Pennsylvania. The Gruvers lived in Sigel, fifteen miles northeast of Clarion. As far as their partnership was concerned, D. H. handled the business aspects while Jesse did the drilling. Clark Gruver said his father was surprised by Slick's anger over the suggestion that oil would not be found at the Wheeler well. Slick was quite adamant, and it seemed as though he was commanding them to find oil. Clark said his father had no further dealings with Slick until about 1928, when he asked him for a drilling job. Slick replied that he was overextended and overworked already and just did not have any wells Gruver could drill. Clark Gruver interview, Tulsa, Okla., July 13, 1989; May Gruver interview, Augusta, Kans., July 13, 1989.

36. Mapes, letter to Dott, July 7, 1944.

37. *Cushing Independent*, February 29, 1912.

38. Ibid., February 8, 1912.

39. Ibid., February 29, 1912.

40. *Oil and Gas Journal*, March 21, 1912, 14.

41. Newsom, *Drumright!*, 19, 20, 22.

42. *Bristow Record*, March 22, 1912.

43. *Cushing Independent*, March 21, 1912; *Oil and Gas Journal*, March 21, 1912, 14.

44. *Drumright Derrick*, June 20, 1984. Her sister, Birdie Wheeler Smith, corroborated this story in, Newsom, *Drumright!*, 21. In a slightly different version, driller R. J. Wallace claims that although Slick was usually at the well he was not there the day the well "blew in." He stated that someone went to tell Slick of the well's completion, and after this Slick rushed to the Wheeler home. Wallace also claimed that the fence around the well was not constructed until that same day. (For this account see *Cushing Daily Citizen*, September 8, 1952.)

45. *Cushing Daily Citizen*, March 19, 1952.

46. Fay Robb Frazier gave this eyewitness account in Newsom, *Drumright!*, 22–23.

47. *Cushing Independent,* March 21, 1912.

48. Writers repeated and embellished this story in numerous works (see note 31 above). Those closest to the truth were *Tulsa Daily World,* March 20, 1912; *Cushing Independent,* March 21, 1912; and Newsom, *Drumright!,* 19–22. One source that actually names a person who leased his livery rig to Slick can be found in the W. D. Grisso Collection—a speech titled "History of Oil Exploration in Oklahoma," dated October 27, 1964, Box 18, Western History Collections, Norman, Okla.

49. *Cushing Daily Citizen,* March 9, 1952.

50. Wood, "Oil and Gas Development," 14; Newsom, *Drumright!,* 19.

51. *Yale Record,* March 21, 1912.

52. "Cushing Field," notes by Ruth Sheldon Knowles for *Greatest Gamblers,* in the DAR Collection, Cushing Public Library, Cushing, Okla. Sinclair later obtained many of Slick's former leases. In 1915 Slick sold his holdings to Milliken and Slick Oil Company. The next year Milliken sold out to Sinclair for ten million dollars. (See *Tulsa Daily World,* April 28, 1916.)

53. *Cushing Independent,* April 11, 1912. Creek County Court records revealed that between March 6 and April 30, 1912, Slick registered more than forty leases in his name.

54. One dollar per acre was the standard rate; see *Yale Record,* March 21, 1912. For Sinclair's lease payment, see "Cushing Field," notes by Knowles, DAR Collection. For Prairie's lease payment, see *Cushing Independent,* April 18, 1912.

55. *Tulsa Daily World,* January 22, 1913. For more on the fraud, theft, and other criminal actions concerning Indian land rights, see Debo, *And Still the Waters Run.*

56. *Tulsa Daily World,* March 28, 29, 1912.

57. Newsom, *Drumright!,* 23. See also *Cushing Daily Citizen,* March 19, 1952.

58. *Tryon Star,* March 28, 1912.

Chapter 3. "Well, I'll Be D———d!": Tom Slick in the Cushing Field

1. *Tulsa Daily World,* March 29, 1912; *Cushing Democrat,* March 21, 1912.

2. *Cushing Democrat,* March 21, 1912.

3. *Tulsa Daily World,* March 22, 1912.

4. *Cushing Independent,* March 28, 1912.

5. *Bristow Record,* March 29, 1912.

6. *Cushing Independent,* April 18, 1912.

7. Ibid., April 11, 25, 1912.

8. *Tulsa Daily World,* May 10, 1912.

9. *Oil and Gas Journal,* June 20, 1912, 8; *Tulsa Daily World,* June 20, 1912.

10. These citations are a composite of well listings from the *Oil and Gas Journal,* June 27, July 4, 11, 1912.

11. "Bill of Complaint," *C. B. Shaffer v. T. B. Slick and B. B. Jones,* U.S. District Court, Eastern District, Muskogee, Okla., August 2, 1912.

12. "Stipulation for Dismissal," Ibid., September 17, 1912; *Bristow Record,* March 3, 10, 1911; *Cushing Independent,* January 25, 1912; *Daily Oklahoman,* April 19, 1925.

13. *Oil and Gas Journal,* September 5, 1912, 10.

14. "Dismissal," *Shaffer v. Slick.*

15. *Tulsa Daily World,* September 21, 1912.

16. Thomas B. Slick, letter to Mary A. and Flored M. Slick, September 18, 1912; Thomas B. Slick, letter to Mary A. and Flored M. Slick, September 27, 1912. In possession of Charles U. Slick.

17. Tom Slick, Jr., interview, July 30, 1951, Benedum and the Oil Industry Collection, Oral History Research Office, Columbia University, New York, N.Y. He made these four remarks in a very short discussion about the Cushing oil boom and the months prior to his father's trip.

18. *Oil and Gas Journal,* January 23, 1913, 14.

19. *Daily Oklahoman,* March 12, 1916.

20. Tom Slick, letter to Mary and Flo, September 27, 1912; *Clarion Democrat,* June 29, August 31, 1905. Flo managed Tom's personal oil business only, not Hi-Grade Oil. Other women did participate in the oil business; Juanita Oil of Oklahoma was managed entirely by women.

21. Ibid.; *Bristow Record,* March 21, 1913.

22. Tom Slick, letter to Mary and Flo, September 18, 1912. I was unable to determine who "Duff" was.

23. Ibid., September 27, 1912.

24. Ibid.

25. Ibid. Even though the letter was touching as an emotional expression to his mother, he added as the last line to his postscript a parting shot at Shaffer: "A nice well came in today close to a lease of mine, if a few more like this come in Shaffer will lose instead of gain."

26. Jesse G. Slick, letter to Mary A. and Flored M. Slick, September 29, 1912. In possession of Charles U. Slick.

27. F. S. Barde Collection, "Oil fields—Cushing and Drumright," Oklahoma Historical Society, Oklahoma City; *Tulsa Daily World,* December 14, 1912.

28. *Daily Oklahoman,* March 12, 1916; *Oil and Gas Journal,* June 5, 1913, 14.

29. *Bristow Record,* March 21, 1913; *Oil and Gas Journal,* March 13, 1913, 2.

30. Barde Collection.

31. All listings found on the oil page in the *Tulsa Daily World* of the date cited.

32. *Bristow Record,* March 29, 1912.

33. *Oil and Gas Journal,* January 23, 1913, 14. For additional accounts of the rapid and sustained growth of Cushing, see Stewart, "Cushing—The Wonder City"; and Wells, *Young Cushing,* esp. 193–206.

34. Newsom, *Drumright!,* 24. This was the approximate population as of January 1913. When the oil boom peaked in 1915 the estimated population had reached thirty thousand.

35. Barde Collection.

36. Ibid.

37. Shelia Hawkins Collection, Kansas State Historical Society, Topeka.

38. Newsom, *Drumright!,* 42. This book is by far the best on the growth of

Drumright. The term *shotgun house* referred to a narrow, wood-frame house of simple design. These were common in boomtowns because they were inexpensive to build and did not require much space.

39. Blatchley, *Waste,* 40.

40. Ibid., 48–50.

41. Barde Collection.

42. Blatchley, *Waste,* 39–40.

43. Barde Collection.

44. *Oil and Gas Journal,* May 7, 1914, 14. All of this oil was not wasted by Slick; the dam was just constructed near his lease and caught all oil from upstream. One estimate put the total amount skimmed from Tiger Creek at various traps at more than fifty thousand barrels of oil. See *Oil and Gas Journal* April 23, 1914, 10.

45. *Oil and Gas Journal,* May 7, 1914, 8, 14.

46. Virgil Anderson, interview, Oral History Collection, Oklahoma Heritage Association, Oklahoma City, Okla., July 8, 1983.

47. *Daily Oklahoman,* September 19, 1915.

48. *Bristow Record,* July 3, 1914.

49. *Oil and Gas Journal,* July 9, 1914, 16; *Tulsa Daily World,* July 8, 1914.

50. During the Cushing boom the Oklahoma legislature did pass laws defining waste of oil and gas and the corporation commission did have nominal enforcement powers. However, just as Oklahoma enacted these laws the demand for oil increased to meet the shortages created by World War I. Officials tended to overlook violations. The laws remained dormant until the extensive flush production of the 1920s and 1930s. Conservation and Slick's role in this issue will be discussed in chapter 6.

51. *Tulsa Daily World,* October 12, 1911.

52. *Chandler News-Publicist,* March 8, May 3, 1912.

53. *Chandler Review,* March 23, 1912.

54. *Chandler News-Publicist,* April 12, 1912.

55. Ibid., May 10, 1912. Delays were caused by Slick's absence because of his father's death, his attempts to gather more leases, and the first contract being declared invalid by city attorneys.

56. Ibid., May 17, 1912.

57. Ibid., July 12, 1912.

58. Ibid., February 21, April 4, 1913.

59. *Cushing Independent,* July 11, August 1, 1912.

60. Ibid., November 14, 1912.

61. Ibid., December 5, 1912. It is interesting to note that Slick's sister must have worked with Jones, since Tom Slick was absent during much of this venture.

62. *Tulsa Daily World,* July 5, 25, 1913; *Bristow Record,* July 18, 1913.

63. There may have been several reasons for these business ventures by Tom Slick. The key reason for the Chandler well was almost certainly to make some "easy money" and get a tremendous block of acreage from the labor of others. The other deals may have been ideas to raise cash to fund more drilling opportunities. They may have reflected a young man with newly acquired wealth eager to spend his money

or simply attempts by Slick to find work less strenuous since his health had grown increasingly fragile.

64. *Tulsa Daily World,* August 1, 1915; May 20, 1913.

65. Beaton, *Enterprise in Oil,* 133.

66. Ibid.

67. *Tulsa Daily World,* September 3, 1913.

68. Beaton, *Enterprise in Oil,* 133.

69. *Tulsa Daily World,* December 6, 1913.

70. Ibid., December 6, 11, 1913. Slick mistakenly believed that since the Carter deal was never consummated (because the Commissioner of Indian Affairs disapproved the sale) he did not owe McConnell a commission. McConnell sued in federal court and won his 5 percent payment plus $1,000 damages for a total of $76,000. (See *Tulsa Daily World,* December 11, 19, 1913.)

71. A. A. Jones, First Assistant Secretary of Interior to Cato Sells, Commissioner of Indian Affairs, December 19, 1913, Bureau of Indian Affairs, Lease Division Correspondence.

72. These figures based on the Index to Lessees and Lessors, Five Civilized Tribes Agency, Bureau of Indian Affairs, Lease Division; a search of records for U.S. Federal Court, Eastern District, Muskogee, Oklahoma, where Indian-related lawsuits were filed; and a listing of all producing properties in the Cushing field printed in Oklahoma Geological Survey, *Bulletin No. 18.* Court records for Creek County, Sapulpa and Federal Court, Muskogee (now in Fort Worth) were especially revealing regarding assigned leases.

Another reason he avoided some Indian leases, particularly Osage lands, was because they were auctioned to the highest bidder. He seemed unwilling to compete with the huge bids of Marland, Prairie, and others. Records indicated that Slick only drilled one well on Osage land. He obtained this lease on assignment in 1924, and the well came in dry. During the Seminole oil boom Slick took a few Indian leases there also, in his name and by assignment.

73. Dana H. Kelsey, Indian Superintendent to Cato Sells, Commissioner of Indian Affairs, December 3, 1913, Bureau of Indian Affairs, Lease Division Correspondence.

74. Cato Sells, Commissioner of Indian Affairs to Franklin K. Lane, Secretary of Interior, December 19, 1913, Bureau of Indian Affairs, Lease Division Correspondence.

75. Glenn W. Patchett, "The Cushing Oil Field," Oklahoma Historical Data Files, "Cushing Field," Mid-Continent Oil and Gas Association, Tulsa.

76. All listings compiled from the oil pages of the *Tulsa Daily World.*

77. *Cushing Independent,* August 8, 1913; "17-17-7" referred to the section, township, and range of the location.

78. *Bristow Record,* May 29, June 12, 17, 1914; *Tulsa Daily World,* July 15, 1914.

79. *Tulsa Daily World,* August 12, 1914; *Bristow Record,* October 2, 1914.

80. Dana Kelsey, letter to Cato Sells, December 3, 1913, Bureau of Indian Affairs, Lease Division Correspondence; *Oil and Gas Journal,* July 23, 1914, 5. Kelsey

thought that perhaps the transfer should be approved since Carter Oil could operate the leases more fully and thus at a greater profit for the Indians concerned.

81. *Tulsa Daily World,* August 1, 1915; *Daily Oklahoman,* March 12, 1916; Oklahoma Secretary of State, "Articles of Incorporation" files, Oklahoma State Archives, Oklahoma City; E. R. Gillespie, Joseph F. Guffey, Robert Pitcairn, Jr., and C. F. Farren were the four Pittsburgh owners.

82. A. A. Jones, First Assistant Secretary of Interior, letter to Cato Sells, Commissioner of Indian Affairs, July 22, 1915, Bureau of Indian Affairs, Lease Division Correspondence.

83. *Tulsa Daily World,* August 1, 1915, January 1, 1915.

84. Ibid., July 21, 1915.

85. Carney, *Cushing Oil Field,* 7.

Chapter 4. In-Law Entrepreneurs

1. Frates, "Biography," 20–21.

2. Ramona Frates Seeligson, interview by author, San Antonio, Tex., July 29, 1986. Mrs. Seeligson is Berenice's sister.

3. *Springfield (Mo.) Daily Leader,* June 22, 1915.

4. *Springfield (Mo.) Republican,* June 22, 1915.

5. Frates, "Biography," 18–21.

6. Ibid., 21–22.

7. Ibid., 22–23; *Depew Independent,* November 5, 1915. Frates completed the line only as far as Shamrock; then he sold out to the Frisco which then finished the railroad into Drumright.

8. Gibson, *Wilderness Bonanza,* 82–83.

9. Minutes of Board of Directors' and Stockholders' meeting, November 17, 1921, Miami Mineral Belt Railroad Company Records, Western Historical Manuscript Collection, University of Missouri, Rolla (hereafter cited as "Minutes," with appropriate date).

10. Ibid., February 24, 1917. J. H. Grant, an attorney, remained a lifelong friend of Slick and represented him in numerous lawsuits. They became such good friends that Slick made provisions for Grant in his will.

11. Ibid., June 19, 1917.

12. Ibid., March 19, 1917.

13. *Miami Record-Herald,* May 18, June 15, 1917.

14. Frates, "Biography," 25.

15. *Miami Record-Herald,* June 29, 1917.

16. Ibid., July 13, 1917.

17. Ibid., August 10, 1917.

18. Ibid., August 24, October 19, December 7, 1917, January 25, 1918; Frates, "Biography," 25.

19. *Miami Record-Herald,* October 19, 1917.

20. *Douthat (Oklahoma) Independent,* August 9, 1917.

21. Frates, "Biography," 25.

22. Ibid.

23. *Miami Record-Herald,* October 19, 1917.

24. "Minutes," December 19, 1929.

25. Frates, "Biography," 26.

26. *Bristow Record,* March 11, 1920.

27. Ibid., April 1, 1920. This meant that both rails weighed ninety pounds per foot (or forty-five pounds per foot of a single rail). This was a higher grade rail. That used on the Mineral Belt was only sixty-five-pound steel.

28. Ibid., June 24, 1920.

29. *Daily Oklahoman,* September 12, 1920.

30. Ibid.

31. Frates, "Biography," 27.

32. *Tulsa Daily World,* June 24, 1923; "Minutes," August 31, 1923.

33. Frates, "Biography," 27–28.

34. Ibid., 27; "Minutes," July 29, 1929; "Minutes," July 30, 1929. Company records revealed that the other Slick-Frates concerns were in debt to the Mineral Belt for these amounts: Union Transportation Company, $94,968.27; Oklahoma Union Railway, $89,598.40; Slick Townsite Company, $7,003.80; and Interurban Construction Company, $50,100.00. Before selling these holdings (except Slick Townsite Company, which was dissolved) Tom Slick paid off the largest sum with his own money. The other three sums were "forgiven" by the Mineral Belt.

35. *Tulsa Daily World,* April 10, 1912.

36. *Cushing Independent,* April 18, 1912.

37. Newsom, *Drumright II,* 4.

38. *Cushing Independent,* May 30, 1912.

39. Ibid., August 15, 1912; Newsom, *Drumright II,* 4.

40. Frates, "Biography," 24.

41. Ibid., 26.

42. *Bristow Record,* March 11, 1920.

43. Ibid., April 22, 1920.

44. Frates, "Biography," 26; *Tulsa Tribune,* June 21, 1936; *Bristow Record,* March 18, 1920.

45. Morris, *Ghost Towns,* 179; *Bristow Record,* March 11, 1920.

46. *Bristow Record,* April 1, 1920, March 18, 1920.

47. Ibid., June 3, 1920.

48. Ibid., July 8, 1920; *Daily Oklahoman,* September 12, 1920.

49. *Slick Spectator,* October 1, 1920; Morris, *Ghost Towns,* 179.

50. *Tulsa Daily World,* February 18, 1921.

51. *Bristow Record,* June 24, 1920; *Daily Oklahoman,* September 12, 1920.

52. *Bristow Record,* April 22, 1920; *Tulsa Daily World,* February 18, 1921.

53. *Tulsa Daily World,* January 8, 1921.

54. *Oilton Gusher,* February 17, 1921.

55. *Bristow Record,* April 22, 1920.

56. Ibid., September 9, 1920. This article was written by William N. Randolph, a journalist for the *Tulsa Tribune.*

57. Ernest C. (Jack) Weber, letter to editor of the *San Antonio (Tex.) Light,* ca. October 1962, in Thomas B. Slick Collection, Western History Collections, University of Oklahoma, Norman, Okla. Weber wrote this letter shortly after the death of T. B. Slick, Jr., who lived in San Antonio.

58. *Slick Times,* December 31, 1920.

59. Ibid.

60. *Daily Oklahoman,* September 12, 1920. The name Nuyaka has an interesting origin. Creek Indians visited President Washington in New York in 1790 and were impressed with the "magnificence" of the city. When they returned to Georgia they renamed their village. Pronouncing New York as well as they could, it came out as "Nuyaka." Then after the Creek removal to Indian Territory (Oklahoma), they transferred the name to a new site there, as they did for many other towns.

61. Ibid.; Frates, "Biography," 26.

62. *Tulsa Daily World,* August 31, 1922; Morris, *Ghost Towns,* 180.

63. *Kansas City Star,* May 5, 1929.

64. Clifford L. Frates, interview by author, August 8, 1986. Frates is the son of J. A. Frates, Sr. Jones hailed from Kosciusko, Mississippi, only about fifty miles from these plantations.

65. Frates, "Biography," 29; *Yazoo County (Mississippi) News,* November 27, 1916.

66. *Yazoo County News,* July 2, 1917; Clifford L. Frates interview.

67. Frates, "Biography," 30.

68. Craighead, "Cushing-Drumright Oil Rush," 26. Eric Ferren, mayor of Shamrock, told this anecdote to Craighead. "Oklahoma Historical Data: Cushing Field," file at Mid-Continent Oil and Gas Association, Tulsa, Okla.

Chapter 5. "To See the Oil Gush Once More"

The title is a quote that a journalist for the Jennings, Oklahoma, newspaper attributed to Tom Slick as he watched his first Jennings well completed as a gusher. Slick said it made him think of years before "to see the oil gush once more in such quantities." *Jennings News,* November 6, 1919.

1. *Bristow Record,* March 3, 1911.

2. *Tulsa Daily World,* November 4, 1919; *Jennings News,* July 3, November 6, 1919.

3. *Jennings News,* February 19, April 8, May 6, 1920.

4. Ernest C. (Jack) Weber, letter to the editor of the *San Antonio (Tex.) Light,* ca. October 1962, Thomas B. Slick Collection, Western History Collections, University of Oklahoma, Norman, Okla. Some of the punctuation in this letter has been supplied. A few other points of interest about this letter include the fact that Slick hired a taxi cab because he could not drive an automobile. He apparently never learned how. He always took a cab or train, and in later years he hired a full-time

chauffeur. The "AT & SF" referred to the Santa Fe Railroad. "Sawbuck" was a slang term of the day for a ten-dollar bill.

5. *County Liner and Cedar Vale Commercial,* December 24, 1920; February 18, 1921; (hereafter cited as *County Liner*).

6. Ibid., February 4, March 11, 1921; *Tulsa Daily World,* April 12, 1921.

7. *County Liner,* September 23, 1921. Unfortunately, this type of wastage of gas was fairly common for that time.

8. Ibid., February 24, 1922.

9. Kesler, *Oil and Gas Resources,* 27.

10. "Hunch, Backed by Unfailing Courage and Faith Resulted in Discovery of Pioneer Oil Field," *Oil and Gas Journal,* June 8, 1922, 32.

11. *Pioneer Oil Herald,* May 16, 1922; *Tulsa Daily World,* May 27, 1922; *Oil Weekly,* February 25, 1922, 61; March 11, 1922, 33; March 18, 1922, 33.

12. *Pioneer Oil Herald,* May 16, 1922; *Ranger Daily Times,* May 14, 1922.

13. Ibid.

14. House, *Oil Field Fury,* 119. See also *Ranger Daily Times,* May 26, 1922.

15. *Oil Weekly,* June 3, 1922, 8; *Oil and Gas Journal,* June 15, 1922, 1, 36.

16. *Oil and Gas Journal,* June 29, 1922, 28.

17. These figures were calculated from the quarterly production reports published in various issues of the *Oil Weekly.*

18. *Tulsa Daily World,* May 17, 1922; *Oil and Gas Journal,* July 20, 1922, 28.

19. House, *Oil Field Fury,* 120–23; *Cross Plains Review,* May 26, 1922.

20. *Cross Plains Review,* June 9, 1922.

21. Ibid., August 18, September 15, 1922; *Tulsa Daily World,* August 29, 1922.

22. Havins, *Something About Brown,* 126; *Oil Weekly,* September 23, 1922, 62; *Cross Plains Review,* November 10, 1922.

23. Connelley, *History of Kansas,* 3:1319.

24. *Tulsa Daily World,* April 24, 1927.

25. *Tonkawa News,* February 2, March 23, August 17, 1922.

26. Ibid., August 28, 1922.

27. Ibid., February 1, 22, March 15, 1923.

28. Ibid., June 21, 1923.

29. Ibid., March 13, 1924.

30. Ibid., March 27, 1924.

31. *Tulsa Daily World,* April 10, 13, 1924.

32. Ibid., April 9, 1924; *Tonkawa News,* April 10, 1924. The debate centered upon the exact depth of Slick's Endicott No. 1 and if the sand encountered was the Bartlesville or the Wilcox.

33. *Tonkawa News,* April 24, May 1, 1924.

34. *Tulsa Daily World,* April 9, 1924.

35. *Oil Weekly,* April 26, 1924, 49.

36. *Tonkawa News,* September 18, 1924.

37. Ibid., September 11, 18, October 23, 1924.

38. Ibid., January 28, 1926.

39. George Bruce, interview by author, Wichita, Kans., July 24, 1989. Bruce, president of Aladdin Petroleum in Wichita, also knew Tom Slick and had business dealings with him in the late 1920s, when Slick returned to play a role in Kansas oil once again.

40. *Wetumka Gazette*, February 29, 1924.

41. *Oil Weekly*, August 8, 1924, 47.

42. *Okemah Ledger*, October 16, 1924.

43. *Wetumka Gazette*, August 22, 1924.

44. *Tulsa Daily World*, November 19, 1924.

45. *Okfuskee County News*, January 15, 1925.

46. *Weleetka American*, February 5, 1925.

47. *Tulsa Daily World*, October 30, 1924; *Oxford Register*, April 24, June 19, 1924.

48. *Tulsa Daily World*, November 1, 1924.

49. *Oxford Register*, October 2, 1924.

50. *Winfield Daily Courier*, October 29, 1924.

51. Ibid. This pipeline was completed two weeks later and pumped the oil from the Slick-Carson pool into the main Marland line at the Graham pool, five miles southeast (see *Oxford Register*, November 13, 1924).

52. *Oxford Register*, October 30, 1924.

53. Ibid., November 6, 1924; *Winfield Daily Courier*, October 31, 1924.

54. *Tulsa Daily World*, November 10, 1924.

55. *Winfield Daily Courier*, October 31, 1924.

56. Kesler, *Oil and Gas Resources*, 22.

57. *Kansas City Star*, May 5, 1929.

58. Ibid.; *Tulsa Daily World*, November 30, 1924.

59. *Tulsa Daily World*, November 30, 1924.

60. *Cushing Independent*, September 22, 1916. Urschel's role as Slick's manager, especially during the years 1916–1924, remains unclear.

61. *Tulsa Daily World*, November 30, 1924.

62. Ibid.

63. Ibid.

64. *Kansas City Star*, May 5, 1929.

65. Ibid.

66. Virtually any newspaper or oil journal consulted for any date from 1920 to 1930 carried reports on Slick's wells.

67. *Fairview Republican*, May 7, 1926.

68. Ibid., August 20, 1926.

69. Ibid., November 5, December 3, 24, 1926.

70. *Kansas City Star*, May 5, 1929.

71. Secretary of State (Oklahoma), *Articles of Incorporation*, Oklahoma Department of Libraries, Archives and Records Division, Oklahoma City, Okla. Tom Slick, Inc., was incorporated May 27, 1926.

72. Charles Mee, interview by author, Oklahoma City, Okla., June 27, 1986. Mee worked for Tom Slick's oil business from 1930 to 1933.

73. Olien and Olien, *Wildcatters,* 28–35.

Chapter 6. "Seminole Is the Greatest Pool of Oil Ever Discovered"

1. *Wewoka Capital-Democrat,* April 19, 1923.
2. Ibid., July 12, 1923.
3. Ibid., September 6, 1923.
4. Ibid., December 6, 1923. Welsh, Townes, and Morris, *History of the Greater Seminole Oil Field,* 8, 16–26.
5. *Tulsa Daily World,* January 18, 1925.
6. Grim, *Recent Oil and Gas Prospecting,* 61, 63, 65.
7. *Kansas City Star,* May 5, 1929.
8. *Tulsa Daily World,* January 20, 1927.
9. Ibid., November 13, 1926; January 21, 22, April 13, 1927.
10. *Kansas City Star,* May 5, 1929.
11. *Seminole Morning News,* June 13, 1928; Welsh, *Greater Seminole,* 56–57.
12. Hazlett, "Property Rights," 32–34.
13. Ibid., 39–40; Clark, "Conservation."
14. *Oklahoma Statutes,* 228.
15. Clark, "Conservation," 386.
16. Turner, "Regulation," 147–48.
17. Slick, "Business Methods," 12.
18. For example, he missed the May 12, 1927, meeting (see *Oil Weekly,* May 20, 1927, 26, 46); *Oil and Gas Journal,* July 21, 1927, 34–35.
19. *Oil and Gas Journal,* July 21, 1927, 34–35.
20. *Seminole Morning News,* August 8, 1928.
21. *Oil Weekly,* September 14, 1928, 28.
22. *Daily Oklahoman,* March 31, 1929; *Oklahoma City Times,* August 16, 1930.
23. See for example *Oil Weekly,* February 22, 1929, 67; *Harlow's Weekly,* April 6, 1929, 5; *Oklahoma City Times,* August 16, September 24, 1930; *Seminole Morning News,* February 17, 1929; and *Daily Oklahoman,* March 31, 1929.
24. *Oklahoma City Times,* August 16, 1930.
25. See various issues of *Oil Weekly* from February to July 1929.
26. *Oklahoma City Times,* August 16, 1930.
27. *Seminole Morning News,* October 6, 1928.
28. *Oil Weekly,* September 14, 1928, 28.
29. *Seminole Morning News,* October 6, 1928.
30. Ibid., October 22, 1929; February 2, 1929. After Slick's death, Urschel and others in the company continued to support proration as a means of conservation. In December 1930, "Thomas B. Slick Interests" printed a full-page advertisement entitled "*Proration Our Salvation*" in an Oklahoma City newspaper (see *Daily Oklahoman,* December 21, 1930.) In 1932 a geologist for Slick-Urschel Oil read a

paper before the American Association of Petroleum Geologists in which he stated, "The value of proration as a conservation measure is indisputable." See Thomas, "Proration."

31. *Oil Weekly,* February 22, 1929, 77.

32. Slick, "Business Methods," 12–13.

33. Ibid.

34. Ibid.

35. Ibid.

36. Mid-Continent Oil and Gas Association [MCO&GA], *Unitization,* 15–16.

37. Hazlett, "Property Rights," 41–43.

38. Buckley, *Petroleum Conservation,* vii–ix, 276–96.

39. Clark, *Oil Century,* 183. The case from which this quotation came was *C. C. Julian Oil and Royalties Company v. Capshaw et al.,* 145 Oklahoma 237.

40. *Ada Evening News,* June 24, 1927.

41. Ibid., June 27, 1927.

42. Ibid., June 26, 27, 1927; *Central Oklahoma Oil Review,* July 4, 1927.

43. *Ada Evening News,* July 3, 1927; *Oil Weekly,* July 1, 1927, 35–36; Secretary of State (Oklahoma), *Articles of Incorporation,* Oklahoma Department of Libraries, Archives and Records Division, Oklahoma City, Okla. Conservation Oil Company was formally chartered on July 5, 1927.

44. *Ada Evening News,* July 3, 1927.

45. Jack T. Conn, letter to Kenny Franks, September 25, 1978, in possession of Kenny Franks, Oklahoma Heritage Association, Oklahoma City, Okla.; William B. Osborn, Jr., interview, July 17, 1978, Oral History Collection, Oklahoma Heritage Association, Oklahoma City, Okla.

46. For more on this topic see Walker, *History.*

47. Slick, "Business Methods," 12–13.

48. *Oil and Gas Journal,* January 19, 1928, 149. Some of those in attendance included James A. Veasey, vice president and chief counsel for Carter Oil; Mark McGee, former adjutant general for Texas; Ray M. Collins, Seminole umpire; Dana H. Kelsey, vice president and general manager of Prairie Oil and Gas; E. B. Reeser, president of Barnsdall Oil; and Henry McGraw, vice president of Gypsy Oil.

49. Ibid.

50. *Shawnee Morning News,* April 25, 1929. Wells drilled by the group still bore the name of the landowner, but "Community" was added as a prefix to the well name. For example, the discovery well was the Community Strothers No. 1. This was often the practice in naming wells drilled on unitized land.

51. MCO&GA, *Unitization,* 22–23.

52. Ibid., 24; *Oil Weekly,* May 23, 1930, 58.

53. *Guthrie Daily Leader,* July 19, 1924; *Cimarron Valley Clipper,* May 6, 1926; February 24, 1927; February 23, 1928; March 20, 1930.

Chapter 7. "Within a Year, I'll Be Back on Top"

1. *Konowa Leader,* August 30, 1928; see also *Kansas City Star,* May 5, 1929; *Daily Oklahoman,* March 21, 1929.

2. Betty S. Moorman scrapbook, unidentified clippings; *Oil Weekly,* March 22, 1929, 60; Merlin Cook, interview by author, San Antonio, Tex., August 8, 1986. Cook began working for Slick in February 1930. He stated that Slick often arose at 2:00 A.M. to visit his wells and monitor progress.

3. *Oil Weekly,* March 22, 1929, 60.

4. *Tecumseh County Democrat,* March 22, 1929.

5. Moorman scrapbook.

6. *Oil Weekly,* March 22, 1929, 60.

7. For examples see ibid.; *Kansas City Star,* May 5, 1929; *Daily Oklahoman,* March 21, 1929.

8. *Tecumseh County Democrat,* March 22, 1929; Moorman scrapbook; *Kansas City Star,* May 5, 1929; *Kansas City Times,* August 16, 1930.

9. *Kansas City Star,* May 5, 1929.

10. This letter was printed in the *Takeoff* 4, no. 10 (August 1930): 1. This publication was the newsletter of the Mid-Continent Map Company.

11. *Wichita Beacon,* March 31, 1929; *Oil Weekly,* April 5, 1929, 72; Moorman scrapbook.

12. Tom Pryor, interview by author, Wichita, Kans., July 13, 1989. Pryor is the son of Ralph Pryor. His sister, Elinor Pryor, wrote a novel entitled *The Big Play* (New York: McGraw Hill, 1951), which was loosely based on the drilling careers of Pryor and Lockhart. Interestingly, Tom Slick is barely mentioned in the book.

13. David Lockhart, interview by author, Casper, Wyo., July 13, 1989. Lockhart, a lease man, is the son of Floyd Lockhart. He said his father told him that Tom Slick's favorite quip was "when you drill a dry hole, start three more wells."

14. George Bruce, interviews by author, Wichita, Kans., August 8, 1986, July 24, 1989.

15. Ibid.; *Oil Weekly,* January 11, 1929, 44.

16. Bruce interview, July 24, 1989.

17. *Wichita Beacon,* March 31, 1929.

18. *Russell Record,* April 1, 1929.

19. Ibid., June 24, 1929; Owen, *Trek of the Oil Finders,* 546–48.

20. *Oil Weekly,* August 16, 1929, 52; October 11, 1929, 192–93.

21. *Great Bend Tribune,* August 6, 1929.

22. Owen, *Trek of the Oil Finders,* 546–48.

23. *McPherson Daily Republican,* October 23, 29, 1929. According to Ira Rinehart (*Kansas Oil,* 83), this was the codiscovery well of the Voshell pool.

24. Rinehart, *Kansas Oil,* 84; *Oil Weekly,* December 13, 1929, 277.

25. Rinehart, *Kansas Oil,* 7. After Slick's death SP&L discovered the Heiken

pool in southwestern Ellsworth County, which was the first commercial producer for that county in October 1930 (ibid., 53); the Orth pool in Rice County on July 9, 1932 (ibid., 67); and the Breford pool, on the border between Ellsworth and Barton Counties, in September 1932 (ibid., 33).

26. Pryor interview, July 13, 1989.

27. *Oil Weekly,* April 5, 1929, 72. Arthur A. Seeligson, Jr., interview by author, San Antonio, Tex., July 29, 1986. Seeligson's father was an executor of Slick's estate, his brother-in-law, and a partner of SRC.

28. Gardner, *Oil and Gas Fields,* 92. For listings on Slick's scattered Texas completions see the *Oil Weekly,* May 30, 1930, 53; June 6, 1930, 82; June 27, 1930, 90; July 4, 1930, 90; July 25, 1930, 84; August 1, 1930, 244; August 8, 1930, 84.

29. Secretary of State (Oklahoma), *Articles of Incorporation,* Oklahoma Department of Libraries, Archives and Records Division, Oklahoma City, Okla.; Moorman scrapbook.

30. *Oil Weekly,* May 10, 1929, 71.

31. *Shawnee Morning News,* May 21, 28, 1929; June 7, 14, 27, 1929; July 1, 1929.

32. "History of Oklahoma City Field," Charles N. Gould Collection, Western History Collections, University of Oklahoma, Norman, Okla.

33. Cornell, *Oil Fever,* 40.

34. Doris Cornell, interview by author, Oklahoma City, Okla., July 18, 1986.

35. Cornell, *Oil Fever,* 40.

36. Gould Collection.

37. All figures compiled from issues of the *Oil and Gas Journal, Oil Weekly,* and the *Daily Oklahoman.* Some of these wells were drilled in partnership with other firms or individuals, but Slick was the primary owner.

38. *Daily Oklahoman,* August 24, 1930.

39. Charles Mee, interview by author, Oklahoma City, Okla., June 27, 1986.

40. Ibid.

41. *Kansas City Star,* May 5, 1929; *Oil Weekly,* January 10, 1930, 53.

42. Miscellaneous civil cases versus T. B. Slick or T. B. Slick, et al., all found in Civil Cases Docket, Oklahoma County Court, Oklahoma City, Okla. Slick had a total of sixty-three lawsuits naming him as the defendant or codefendant.

43. *Bristow Record,* August 16, 1930. Slick had known Hughes for years. When Slick departed for his world tour in 1912, Jesse Slick and Hughes managed Slick's drilling activities in the Cushing field.

44. *Oklahoma News,* January 19, 20, 1931.

45. *Bristow Record,* August 16, 1930.

46. According to the drilling reports published in the *Daily Oklahoman,* August 10, 1930, Slick and Slick with partners owned 47 of the 329 wells in the Oklahoma City field. Thus Slick accounted for 14 percent of all drilling activity in the field. Wirt Franklin (and Franklin with others) was the nearest independent competitor with about 6 percent of the wells.

47. *Oklahoma City Times,* August 16, 1930.

Chapter 8. "My Whole Life Has Been Work, Work, Work"

1. *Tulsa Tribune,* August 17, 1930.

2. Thomas B. Slick, "Last Will and Testament," July 15, 1930 (hereafter cited as TBS Will), Thomas B. Slick Collection, Western History Collections, Norman, Okla. (hereafter cited as TBS Collection).

3. *Tulsa Tribune,* August 17, 1930; *McAlester Democrat,* August 21, 1930; Slick may have been plagued by thyroid problems and associated ailments most of his life. His goiter was the exophthalmic variety, which meant that his thyroid gland produced too much of the hormone thyroxine. This problem is characterized by a high metabolic rate, nervousness, high blood pressure, and associated heart irregularities. Slick manifested these problems all of his life. His thin physique might have been attributable, in part, to his fast metabolism and constant work. Nervousness was clearly one of his traits. In his letter to his mother in 1912, Slick told her that his doctor had warned him about his heart and his need for a long rest. He may also have had high blood pressure. The fact that he smoked heavily also contributed to his poor health. In his overall condition, Slick may have worked himself to death, as many people believed at the time.

4. *Tulsa Tribune,* August 17, 1930; *Muskogee Phoenix,* August 19, 1930.

5. *Daily Oklahoman,* August 17, 1930; *Oklahoma City Times,* August 18, 1930.

6. *Daily Oklahoman,* August 24, 1930.

7. *Cimarron Valley Clipper,* August 21, 1930.

8. The First National Bank and Trust and the City of Guthrie resolutions were found in the Betty S. Moorman scrapbook; the Oklahoma City Producers Association statement can be found in the *Daily Oklahoman,* August 24, 1930.

9. Kirkpatrick's first poem was a highly emotional and deeply sentimental ode entitled "To Tom Slick." The second poem, "Geese Flying South," reflected upon the days when Slick and his friends would travel to Rockport, Texas, for their annual hunting trip. Both poems were printed in Oklahoma newspapers but were later published in an unusual book with handmade wooden covers and leather bindings; Kirkpatrick and Holding, *Dim Trails* 9, 27–29.

10. For generally negative comments see *Altus Times-Democrat,* August 19, 1930; *Kansas City Star,* September 4, 1930; *Blue Valley Farmer,* November 20, 1930; *Chickasha Star,* September 4, 1930. These newspapers all suggested that Slick had a social obligation to leave his money to charity.

11. TBS Will.

12. Slick's eldest son had changed his middle name from Bernard to Baker after the family had a falling-out with B. B. Jones.

13. TBS Will.

14. *Muskogee Times-Democrat,* August 26, 1930. See also *Tulsa Tribune,* August 27, 1930.

15. *Tulsa Tribune,* August 23, 1930.

16. *U.S. Statutes at Large,* v. 44, part 2, (Washington, D.C.: Government Printing Office, 1927), 69–70; White, "State Inheritance Tax Laws," 625–27; Linn L. Reist,

letter to Harry E. Rugh, September 29, 1930, TBS Collection; Estate of Thomas B. Slick, Valuation Report, October 10, 1932 (hereafter cited as Valuation Report), TBS Collection.

17. *Tulsa Tribune*, August 27, 1930.

18. *Compiled Oklahoma Statutes*, 1921, Section 9916. Cited in Memo For Mr. King: Statutory Provisions which set out the Duties of the Attorney General in the Collection of the Inheritance Tax. In Attorney General, Civil Cases, File No. 7960, Oklahoma Department of Libraries, Archives and Records Division, Oklahoma City, Okla. (hereafter cited as Atty. Gen. File).

19. *William H. Murray v. A.S.J. Shaw, Frank C. Carter, and Executors and Trustees of the T.B. Slick Estate,* Oklahoma County Court, Oklahoma City, Okla.

20. On September 12, 1930, Shaw and Robertson, considering Slick to be a nonresident, signed a contract that authorized Robertson to collect the Slick taxes for Oklahoma. King refused to give his approval (which was required to validate the contract) and wrote to Robertson informing him that the attorney general believed Slick was a resident; J. Berry King, letter to J.B.A. Robertson, September 12, 1930, Atty. Gen. File.

21. J. Berry King, letter to William H. Murray, January 6, 1931, Atty. Gen. File.

22. William J. Holloway, letter to J. Berry King, January 8, 1931, Atty. Gen. File.

23. Separate Answer of J. Berry King, Attorney General of the State of Oklahoma, re *Murray v. Shaw, et al.,* Atty. Gen. File.

24. *Tulsa Daily World*, January 9, 1931. Murray, in his memoirs, remembered, "I went to the banquet, not knowing whether the Court would fine me for contempt, but I was ready to go to jail rather than betray, and remain there and take the oath of office on the day under the Constitution and then call out the Guards to liberate me." He then, with an apparent lapse of memory, noted, "But the court did the right thing and never bothered me." This, of course, ignored the fact that he had been subpoenaed, and he had the charges dismissed. See Murray, *Memoirs,* 2:399.

25. *Oklahoma City Times*, January 9, 1931.

26. *Oklahoma News*, January 9, 1931.

27. *Tulsa Tribune*, January 9, 1931; J. Berry King, letter to Oklahoma Tax Commission, July 11, 1931, Atty. Gen. File.

28. *Oklahoma News*, January 10, 1931.

29. Ibid.

30. *Daily Oklahoman*, January 15, 1931.

31. Motion of the State of Oklahoma to Revoke the Order or Decree of Court Probating the Will of Thomas B. (T. B.) Slick, Deceased, As a Foreign Will, Oklahoma County Court, TBS Collection.

32. TBS Will.

33. Unidentified newspaper clipping in Atty. Gen. File. The file also contained a copy of the affidavit and the charter of incorporation.

34. Harry E. Rugh, letter to W. N. Stokes, June 8, 1931, TBS Collection.

35. *W. A. Field v. T. B. Slick*, Oklahoma County Court.

36. *William Hassell v. T. B. Slick, et al.*, Oklahoma County Court. Federal courts have jurisdiction when a citizen of one state sues a citizen of another.

37. *Eva Richards v. Rebecca Huff*, Supreme Court of Oklahoma, Oklahoma City, Okla. In this case, J. C. Huff, a professional gambler turned oilman, had lived in Oklahoma but claimed Texas as his residence. The court agreed for the reasons cited in the text.

38. See W. N. Stokes, letter to Harry E. Rugh, January 16, 1931; Rugh, letter to Stokes, January 22, 1931; Stokes, letter to Rugh, January 28, 1931; Rugh, letter to Stokes, February 4, 1931, all found in TBS Collection.

39. W. T. McConnell, letter to William H. Murray, March 20, 1931, Atty. Gen. File.

40. Thirteenth Legislature of the State of Oklahoma. *Journal of the House of Representatives Regular Session,* vol. 2, (House Bill #486), 1998–99; Thirteenth Legislature of the State of Oklahoma, *Journal of the Senate,* 2158, 2164, 2171, 2252–53, 2281–83, 2295, 2337, 2424; and State of Oklahoma, *Session Laws of 1931,* 232–35.

41. *Daily Oklahoman,* May 8, 1931.

42. Melven Cornish, letter to J. Berry King, July 8, 1931, TBS Collection.

43. J. Berry King, letter to Oklahoma Tax Commission, July 11, 1931, Atty. Gen. File.

44. See for example *Daily Oklahoman,* January 7, 1932; *Blackwell Morning Tribune,* January 8, 1932; *Blue Valley Farmer,* January 7, 14, 1932.

45. Order Appointing Inheritance Tax Appraisers, Oklahoma County Court; TBS Collection.

46. Valuation Report, TBS Collection.

47. Raymond F. Kravis, interview by author, Tulsa, Okla., September 26, 1986. Kravis helped with evaluating the oil properties of the Slick estate. He believed the fact that the IRS accepted the appraisal value left Oklahoma little choice but to go along with the same figure.

48. W. N. Stokes, letter to Robert M. Rainey, September 26, 1932, TBS Collection.

49. Robert M. Rainey, telegram to Phillip S. Moyer, September 26, 1932, TBS Collection. Moyer was the deputy attorney general for Pennsylvania.

50. Robert M. Rainey, letter to W. N. Stokes, September 28, 1932, TBS Collection.

51. Hearing In the Matter of the Estate of Thomas B. (T. B.) Slick, Deceased, Oklahoma County Court, Oklahoma City, Okla.

52. Olien and Olien, *Wildcatters,* chs. 1–3.

53. Ibid., 3, 10; Olien and Olien, *Easy Money,* 54.

54. Many of the sources cited for chapters 2 and 3 of this work can be consulted in this regard. Stories about Slick may also be found in the Oral History Collection at the Oklahoma Heritage Association, and in the Living Legends Collection and the Oral History Collection at the Oklahoma Historical Society.

Epilogue

1. *Daily Oklahoman,* January 24, 1931; Raymond F. Kravis, interview by author, Tulsa, Okla., September 26, 1986; Gorman, *Petroleum Directory;* Tom Pryor, interview by author, Wichita, Kans., July 13, 1989.

2. Kirkpatrick, *Crimes' Paradise.*

3. Slick, "Some Comments."

4. Gardner, *Reference Report,* 6, 26–27, 62.

5. *Kansas City Star,* February 22, 1948.

6. Tom Slick, Jr., interview, July 30, 1951, Benedum and the Oil Industry Collection, Oral History Research Office, Columbia University, New York, N.Y.

7. *San Antonio Express-News,* October 25, 1981; Presley, *Saga of Wealth,* 358–61; Coleman, *Tom Slick and Yeti.* The two books by Tom Slick, Jr., concerning world peace were *The Last Great Hope* (San Antonio: Naylor, 1951) and *Permanent Peace: A Check and Balance Plan* (Englewood Cliffs, N.J.: Prentice Hall, 1958).

8. "Slick Brothers"; Slick, "Comments."

9. Betty Slick Moorman, interview by author, San Antonio, Tex., July 28, 1986.

Glossary

This glossary provides brief definitions for some of the oil and legal terms used in the text. Several of these entries were derived from Carl Coke Rister's *Oil! Titan of the Southwest* and Edgar Wesley Owen's *Trek of the Oil Finders*.

BARREL: Standard measurement for oil. One barrel equals forty-two gallons.

CABLE-TOOL RIG: Type of drilling rig using a cable suspended from the top of the derrick to lift and drop a drilling tool into the well. The cable can be extended as the well deepens or reeled in (much like a fishing reel) to withdraw the tools from the well. Cable-tool rigs literally pounded and chiseled the well to completion.

FIELD: An area characterized by having several oil pools in the general vicinity.

FLUSH PRODUCTION: The early production from an oil pool before the natural pressure is dissipated by waste of gas and/or overdrilling. During this time larger profits are generally made because the wells are under natural flow. After the period of flush production the operator must pay the increased costs of pumping the oil to the surface.

GRAVITY: The weight of oil at a certain temperature. Different geologic formations produce oil which may vary in viscosity, chemical content, etc. Oil with a higher gravity generally is worth more because a greater number of products can be refined from it.

INDEPENDENTS: Single-proprietor oil operations. These entrepreneurs generally engaged in only one aspect of the oil business, usually production. They had the advantages of personal involvement, maneuverability, and low overhead, and could profitably operate properties on which the majors would lose money. Disadvantages included the fact that they often had to depend on others for transporting their oil and they generally had less operating capital.

INITIAL PRODUCTION: The initial flow of oil from a new well. In a short time, the flow stabilizes and is usually at a lower rate.

MID-CONTINENT: A large, prolific oil region underlying much of Oklahoma, Kansas, central and east Texas, Louisiana, and southwestern Arkansas.

NATURAL FLOW: When a well flows without the assistance of an air lift, or anything other than natural pressure within the sand.

OFFSET WELL: A well on one lease drilled to offset a well on an adjacent lease to capture the leaseholder's rightful part of oil in the common oil pool before it "migrates" to the neighboring well.

PAY SAND: The oil-bearing sand or strata that the driller sought.

PINCHING DOWN (or choking): Restricting the flow of oil from a well.

POOL: An underground accumulation of oil in a single and separate reservoir (ordinarily a porous sandstone or limestone). In a real sense, oil is not found in subsurface pools or lakes as formerly believed.

PRORATION: Regulations that required an operator to reduce the production from a well or wells, usually on a proportional basis.

ROTARY RIG: A drilling rig that rotates or spins a string of pipe with a drill bit attached to the end. Came into general use in the late 1920s. These rigs had the advantage of being much faster than cable-tool rigs, but they cost much more to operate.

SAND: An underground formation that contains oil and/or natural gas. Actually these minerals are found in layers of porous rock, but "sand" helps convey the idea more easily. Sands are found in varying depths, and the oil contained therein has different characteristics. Sands generally bear the name of the discoverer or the location where drillers first found the sand. Examples include Wilcox sand, Bartlesville sand, and Layton sand.

SHOOT: To discharge nitroglycerin in a well. This dangerous task was performed by a shooter, who would place the nitroglycerin inside a tube known as a torpedo. He then lowered the container into the well to the desired depth and detonated the substance with an electrical charge. The explosion fractured the sand or rock and enabled the oil to flow.

SHOWING OF OIL OR GAS: Drillers examined the cuttings or debris that rose to the surface while they were drilling the well. By inspecting these cuttings and by knowing the depth of the well, the driller could determine the geologic formation in which he was drilling. Sometimes these cuttings had traces of oil, which of course informed the driller that he was getting close to completion.

SPUD IN: To begin drilling a well.

STAR RIG: A small, portable drilling rig, used exclusively for shallow wells.

UNITIZATION: Consolidating separately owned leases into one block of acreage and treating it as a single unit for the purposes of profitable and efficient development; expenses and profit are shared proportionally by the various owners.

WELL LOG: A driller's detailed record of the formations encountered in the drilling of a well.

WELL SPACING: Placing a minimal number of wells on a block of acreage so as to reduce waste and to avoid over drilling.

WILDCATTER: An oil operator who leases and drills for oil in unproven territory, generally considered to be one mile or more from an area that has production.

Bibliography

Published Sources

Ashley, George H., and J. French Robinson. *Oil and Gas Fields of Pennsylvania*. Vol. 1. Harrisburg: J. L. L. Kuhn, 1922.

Ball, Max W. *This Fascinating Oil Business*. New York: Bobbs-Merrill, 1940.

Beaton, Kendall. *Enterprise in Oil: A History of Shell in the United States*. New York: Appleton-Century-Crofts, 1957.

Blatchley, Raymond S. *Waste of Oil and Gas in the Mid-Continent Fields*. Bureau of Mines, Technical Paper No. 45. Washington, D.C.: Government Printing Office, 1913.

Buckley, Stuart E., ed. *Petroleum Conservation*. Dallas: E. J. Storm, 1951.

Carll, John F. *The Geology of the Oil Regions of Warren, Venango, Clarion, and Butler Counties*. Harrisburg: Board of Commissioners for the Second Geological Survey, 1880.

———. *The Oil and Gas Fields of Western Pennsylvania*. Harrisburg: Board of Commissioners for the Geological Survey, 1890.

Carney, George O. *Cushing Oil Field: Historic Preservation Survey*. Stillwater: Oklahoma State University, Department of Geography, 1981.

Clark, Blue. "The Beginning of Oil and Gas Conservation in Oklahoma, 1907–1931." *Chronicles of Oklahoma* 55 (Winter 1977–1978): 375–91.

Clark, J. Stanley. *The Oil Century: From the Drake Well to the Conservation Era*. Norman: University of Oklahoma Press, 1958.

Coleman, Loren. *Tom Slick and the Search for the Yeti*. Boston: Faber and Faber, 1989.

Connelley, William E. *History of Kansas, State and People: Kansas at the First Quarter Post of the Twentieth Century.* 3 vols. Chicago: American Historical Society, 1928.

Cornell, Doris. *Oil Fever: The Biography of John R. Bunn.* Oklahoma City: Oklahoma Heritage Association, 1985.

Craighead, David. "The Cushing-Drumright Oil Rush." *Oklahoma Today* 16 (Spring 1966): 24–26.

Debo, Angie. *And Still the Waters Run.* Princeton, N.J.: Princeton University Press, 1940.

Duncan, Bob. *The Dicky Bird Was Singing: Men, Women, and Black Gold.* New York: Rinehart, 1952.

Forbes, Gerald. "The Passing of the Small Oil Man." *Southern Economic Journal* 7 (October 1940): 204–15.

Gardner, Frank J. *Reference Report on Oil and Gas Fields of the Texas Lower Gulf Coast.* Dallas: Five Star Oil Report, 1951.

Getty, J. Paul. *My Life and Fortunes.* New York: Duell, Sloan, and Pearce, 1963.

Gibson, Arrell Morgan. *Wilderness Bonanza: The Tri-State District of Missouri, Kansas, and Oklahoma.* Norman: University of Oklahoma Press, 1972.

Gorman, B. R. *Gorman's Petroleum Directory of Oklahoma.* Tulsa: Anderson Printing, 1937.

Grim, Ralph E. *Recent Oil and Gas Prospecting in Mississippi with a Brief Study of Subsurface Geology.* Jackson: Mississippi State Geological Survey, 1928.

Havins, T. R. *Something About Brown: A History of Brown County, Texas.* Brownwood, Tex.: Banner Printing, 1958.

Hazlett, George W. "Property Rights and Oil Production." In *Oil for Today—And for Tomorrow* (Oklahoma City: Interstate Oil Compact Commission, 1953).

House, Boyce. *Oil Field Fury.* San Antonio: Naylor, 1954.

"Hunch, Backed by Unfailing Courage and Faith Resulted in Discovery of Pioneer Oil Field." *Oil and Gas Journal* 21 (June 8, 1922): 32.

Hurt, Harry, III. *Texas Rich: The Hunt Dynasty from the Early Oil Days through the Silver Crash.* New York: Norton, 1981.

Interstate Oil Compact Commission. *Oil for Today—And for Tomorrow.* Oklahoma City: Interstate Oil Compact Commission, 1953.

Kesler, L. W. *Oil and Gas Resources of Kansas, 1927.* Lawrence: State Geological Survey of Kansas, 1928.

Kirkpatrick, Ernest E. *Crimes' Paradise: The Authentic Inside Story of the Urschel Kidnapping.* San Antonio: Naylor, 1934.

Kirkpatrick, Ernest E., and Vera Holding. *Dim Trails: A Collection of Poems.* Brownwood, Tex.: Ben H. Moore, 1938.

Knowles, Ruth Sheldon. *The Greatest Gamblers: The Epic of American Oil Exploration.* Norman: University of Oklahoma Press, 1978.

"The Magic Knock of Fortune." *Literary Digest,* March 14, 1914, 568, 570, 572.

Mallison, Sam T. *The Great Wildcatter.* Charleston: Education Foundation of West Virginia, 1953.

Mathews, John Joseph. *Life and Death of an Oilman: The Career of E. W. Marland.* Norman: University of Oklahoma Press, 1951.

Mid-Continent Oil and Gas Association. *Handbook on Unitization of Oil Pools.* Tulsa: Mid-Continent Oil and Gas Association, 1930.

Miner, Craig. *Discovery! Cycles of Change in the Kansas Oil and Gas Industry, 1860–1987.* Wichita: Kansas Independent Oil and Gas Association, 1987.

Morris, John W. *Ghost Towns of Oklahoma.* Norman: University of Oklahoma Press, 1977.

Murray, William H. *Memoirs of Governor Murray and True History of Oklahoma.* 3 vols. Boston: Meador, 1945.

Newsom, D. Earl. *Drumright! Glory Days of a Boom Town.* Perkins, Okla.: Evans, 1985.

———. *Drumright II (And Shamrock, Pemeta, Oilton, and Olive): A Thousand Memories.* Perkins, Okla.: Evans, 1987.

Oklahoma Statutes Annotated, Title 52, Oil and Gas. Saint Paul: West, 1969.

Olien, Roger M., and Diana Davids Olien. *Wildcatters: Texas Independent Oilmen.* Austin: Texas Monthly Press, 1984.

———. *Easy Money: Oil Promoters and Investors in the Jazz Age.* Chapel Hill: University of North Carolina Press, 1990.

Owen, Edgar Wesley. *Trek of the Oil Finders: A History of Exploration for Petroleum.* Tulsa: American Association of Petroleum Geologists, 1975.

Presley, James. *A Saga of Wealth: The Rise of the Texas Oilmen.* New York: G. P. Putnam's Sons, 1978.

Rinehart, Ira. *Kansas Oil.* Tulsa: Rinehart Oil News Company, 1936.

Rister, Carl Coke. *Oil! Titan of the Southwest.* Norman: University of Oklahoma Press, 1949.

Ross, J. S. *Preliminary Report on Petroleum Engineering in the Tonkawa Oil Field, Kay and Noble Counties, Oklahoma.* N.p., 1923.

Slick, T. B. "Better Business Methods Instead of State Control Advised for Oil Industry." *Harlow's Weekly,* October 8, 1927, 12–13.

State of Oklahoma. *Session Laws of 1931* (Oklahoma City: Harlow, 1931).

Stewart, Charles I. "Cushing—The Wonder City." *Harlow's Weekly,* June 5, 1915, 378–80.

"The Slick Brothers." *Time,* January 28, 1946, 77–78.

Thoburn, Joseph B., and Muriel H. Wright. *Oklahoma: A History of the State and Its People.* 4 vols. New York: Lewis Historical Publishing, 1929.

Thomas, Harold S. "Proration at Oklahoma City, Oklahoma." *Bulletin of the American Association of Petroleum Geologists* 16 (October 1932): 1021–1028.

U.S. Statutes at Large. v. 44, part 2. Washington, D. C.: Government Printing Office, 1927.

Walker, James P. *A History of the International Petroleum Exposition and Congress, 1923–1979.* Oklahoma City: Oklahoma Heritage Association, 1984.

Wells, Laura Lou. *Young Cushing in Oklahoma Territory.* Perkins, Okla.: Evans, 1985.

Welsh, Louise, Willa Mae Townes, and John W. Morris. *A History of the Greater Seminole Oil Field.* Oklahoma City: Oklahoma Heritage Association, 1981.

Wheaton, George E. *Kansas-Indian Territory Oil and Gas Fields.* Chanute, Kans.: S. N. Francis, 1904.

White, Charles P. "The Effect of the 80 Per Cent Credit Clause of the Federal Estate Tax Law on State Inheritance Tax Laws." *Journal of Political Economy* 36 (October 1928): 625–33.

Williamson, Harold F., et al. *The American Petroleum Industry: The Age of Energy, 1899–1959.* Evanston: Northwestern University Press, 1963.

Wood, Robert H. "Oil and Gas Development in North-Central Oklahoma." In *United States Geological Survey. Bulletin No. 531.* Washington, D.C.: Government Printing Office, 1913.

Unpublished Sources

Anderson, Virgil. Interview. Oral History Collection, Oklahoma Heritage Association, Oklahoma City, Okla., July 8, 1983.

Attorney General Files, Civil Cases, File No. 7960. Archives and Records Division, Oklahoma Department of Libraries, Oklahoma City, Okla.

Barde, F. S. Collection. Oklahoma Historical Society, Oklahoma City, Okla.

Baxter, Al. "Thomas B. Slick." In *Annual Report: The Prairie Oil and Gas Co., Oklahoma City District.* N.p., 1930.

Bruce, George. Interviews by author. Wichita, Kans. August 8, 1986, and July 24, 1989.

Bureau of Indian Affairs. Lease Division Correspondence, Federal Records Center, Fort Worth, Tex.

Civil Cases Docket. Miscellaneous cases versus T. B. Slick or T. B. Slick, et al., Oklahoma County Court, Oklahoma City, Okla.

Conn, Jack T. Letter to Kenny Franks, September 25, 1978. In possession of Kenny Franks, Oklahoma Heritage Association. Oklahoma City, Okla.

Cook, Merlin. Interview by author. San Antonio, Tex., August 8, 1986.

Cornell, Doris. Interview by author. Oklahoma City, Okla. July 18, 1986.

DAR Collection. Cushing Public Library, Cushing, Okla.

Eva Richards v. Rebecca Huff (1930). Supreme Court of Oklahoma, Oklahoma City.

Frates, Clifford L. Interview by author. Oklahoma City, Okla., August 8, 1986.

Frates, Joseph Anthony, Sr. "Biography of Joseph Anthony Frates, Sr." Thomas B. Slick Collection. N.p., n.d.

Gould, Charles N. Collection. Western History Collections, Norman, Okla.

Grisso, W. D. Collection. Western History Collections, Norman, Okla.

Gruver, Clark. Interview by author. Tulsa, Okla., July 13, 1989.

Gruver, May. Interview by author. Augusta, Kans., July 13, 1989.

Index to Lessees and Lessors, Five Civilized Tribes Agency. Federal Records Center, Bureau of Indian Affairs, Lease Division, Oklahoma County Court, Oklahoma City, Okla.

Kelley, Mrs. E. F. Interview. Doris Duke Indian Oral History Collection, Western History Collections, Norman, Okla., June 12, 1967.

Kravis, Raymond F. Interview by author. Tulsa, Okla., September 26, 1986.

Lease Register. Creek County Court, Sapulpa, Okla.

Lockhart, David. Interview by author. Casper, Wyo., July 13, 1989.

McCabe, Gerard B. Letter to author, November 1, 1989. In possession of the author.

Mee, Charles. Interview by author. Oklahoma City, Okla. June 27, 1986.

Miami Mineral Belt Railroad Company Records. Western Historical Manuscript Collection, Rolla, Mo.

Mid-Continent Oil and Gas Association, Tulsa, Okla. "Oklahoma Historical Data—Cushing Field," File.

Moorman, Betty Slick. Interview by author. San Antonio, Tex., July 28, 1986.

Moorman, Betty Slick. Scrapbook of identified clippings, unidentified clippings, and photographs. San Antonio, Tex.

Osborn, William B., Jr. Interview. Oral History Collection, Oklahoma Heritage Association, Oklahoma City, Okla., July 17, 1978.

Platt, Martha Rugh. Interview by author. Minneapolis, Minn., October 21, 1989.

Platt, Martha Rugh. Letter to author, May 13, 1986. In possession of the author.

Pryor, Tom. Interview by author. Wichita, Kans., July 13, 1989.

Secretary of State (Oklahoma). *Articles of Incorporation.* Oklahoma Department of Libraries, Archives and Records Division, Oklahoma City.

Seeligson, Arthur A., Jr. Interview by author. San Antonio, Tex., July 29, 1986.

Seeligson, Ramona Frates. Interview by author. San Antonio, Tex., July 29, 1986.

Showers, Katrina Baker. Letter to Charles F. Urschel, Jr., December 12, 1978. In possession of Charles U. Slick, Atlanta, Ga.

Slick, Charles U. Interview by author. Atlanta, Ga., October 19, 1989.

Slick, Thomas B. Collection. Western History Collections, Norman, Okla.

Slick, Thomas B., Jr. "Some Comments on . . . The Life of Tom Slick, Sr." Speech given at "Old Timers' Dinner," Cushing, Okla., September 9, 1952.

Slick, Tom, Jr. Interview. Benedum and the Oil Industry Collection, Oral History Collection, Columbia University, New York, N.Y., July 30, 1951.

Turner, Alvin O'Dell. "The Regulation of the Oklahoma Oil Industry." Ph.D. diss., Oklahoma State University, 1977.

Index

Tulsa, Oklahoma, 60–61, 102
Tulsa Country Club, 94
Tulsa Daily World, 30, 32, 41, 60, 75
Tulsa Democrat, 30

Union Transportation Company, 60, 61
United States Bureau of Mines, 7
unitization, 90–91, 92, 94, 95, 96, 119
Upton County, Tex., 123
Urschel, Charles F.: as best friend of Slick, 10; kidnapping of, 122; marriage to Flored Slick, 79; marriage to Berenice Slick, 122; as trustee of Slick estate, 101, 108, 121–22; work for Slick, 79, 80, 98, 102
Urschel, Charles F., Jr., 122, 126n. 30

Valley Center, Kans., 100
Valley Plantation, Miss., 66–67
Voshell oil pool, 101

Wacoche, Aggie, 31
Wacoche, Isaac, 49
Wacoche, Johnson, 31, 49
W. A. Field v. T. B. Slick, 113–14, 129n. 2
Walker No. 1 (well), 91–93
Wallace, R. J., 131n. 44
Weaver, Claude, 112
Weber, Ernest C. (Jack), 69
Wellington oil pool, 101
well spacing, 90–91, 92, 94–96, 119
Wentz, Lew, 8, 121

Wentz Oil Company, 94
Wepaco No. 1 (well), 105
West Virginia, petroleum industry in, 6, 11, 15, 28
Wetumka, Okla., 76
Wewoka, Okla., 85, 86
Wewoka oil pool, 86
Wheeler, Frank M., 27, 28, 29
Wheeler Camp, 42
Wheeler sand, 49
Wheeler well, 23, 27–32, 34, 36, 131n. 35
White Sand Oil Company, 16
Wichita, Kans., 99, 100
Wilcox sand, 75, 78, 86
wildcat drilling, 6, 20, 25, 26, 27, 33, 68, 78, 80–81, 85, 90, 91, 97, 98, 100, 105, 121. *See also* Slick, Thomas B.: leasing practices of
wild wells, 104–105
William Hassell v. T. B. Slick, 114
Wilson, Edward R., 71
Wright oil pool, 100
Wrightsman, Charles J.: and Hi-Grade Oil, 26, 37, 40; as partner of Slick, 25, 33, 34, 51, 61; sells holdings to Slick, 102

Yale, Okla., 20, 21
Young County, Tex., 102
Youngstown oil pool, 58

Zapata County, Tex., 102
zinc mining. *See* Tri-State District

LaVergne, TN USA
25 January 2011
213926LV00004B/7/A